Samuel Sharpe

Egyptian Mythology and Egyptian Christianity

With their Influence on the Opinions of Modern Christendom

Samuel Sharpe

Egyptian Mythology and Egyptian Christianity
With their Influence on the Opinions of Modern Christendom

ISBN/EAN: 9783337180362

Printed in Europe, USA, Canada, Australia, Japan

Cover: Foto ©Lupo / pixelio.de

More available books at **www.hansebooks.com**

EGYPTIAN MYTHOLOGY

AND

EGYPTIAN CHRISTIANITY.

Works by the same Author.

THE HISTORY OF EGYPT. 2 vols. 8vo. *Fourth Edition.*

EGYPTIAN INSCRIPTIONS; two hundred and sixteen Plates, in folio.

CHRONOLOGY AND GEOGRAPHY OF ANCIENT EGYPT.

ALEXANDRIAN CHRONOLOGY.

EGYPTIAN HIEROGLYPHICS; with a Vocabulary.

EGYPTIAN ANTIQUITIES IN THE BRITISH MUSEUM.

THE TRIPLE MUMMY CASE OF AROERI-AO.

THE NEW TESTAMENT, TRANSLATED FROM GRIESBACH'S TEXT. *Fifth Edition.*

CRITICAL NOTES ON THE AUTHORIZED ENGLISH VERSION OF THE NEW TESTAMENT.

HISTORIC NOTES ON THE BOOKS OF THE OLD AND NEW TESTAMENTS. 12mo. *Second Edition.*

EGYPTIAN MYTHOLOGY

AND

EGYPTIAN CHRISTIANITY,

WITH THEIR INFLUENCE ON THE OPINIONS
OF MODERN CHRISTENDOM.

BY

SAMUEL SHARPE,

AUTHOR OF "THE HISTORY OF EGYPT."

LONDON:
JOHN RUSSELL SMITH,
36, SOHO SQUARE.
1863.

LONDON:
BOWDEN AND BRAWN, PRINTERS,
13, PRINCES STREET, LITTLE QUEEN STREET, W.C.

CONTENTS.

THE RELIGION OF UPPER EGYPT.

	PAGE		PAGE
The gods created out of visible objects and attributes	2	Their ornaments copied by the Jews	31
The goddesses	5	Their duties	33
Gods who had been mortals	7	Their ventriloquism, serpent-charming, divining	36
Their families	8		
The biography of Osiris	9	Their wives, priestess	38
His birthplace and burial place	10	Their dress, tonsure, offerings	39
Monotheism and polytheism compared	11	The sacrifice of criminals	41
		The pyramids of Memphis and cave tombs of Thebes	42
Their number increased by division and by union	12	That of Oimenepthah I	43
The trinities	14	The love for the gods	44
The animals worshipped	15	The conquest of the serpent of evil	45
Wars about the animals	16		
Worship of Ancestors	17	The mummies	46
Worship of kings	,,	The four gods of the dead	48
Their miraculous birth	18	Ceremonies of burial	49
The sacred tree of life	20	The trial by Osiris	50
Reasons for this worship	,,	The mediators and their atonement	52
The temples described	22		
The intercolumnar separation between priest and laity	24	Two views of the resurrection	53
		The funereal tablets	55
The Priesthood	26	The employments after death	,,
The priests' cells	27	Opinions about the future state borrowed by Greeks	56
The orders of priesthood	29		

THE RELIGION OF LOWER EGYPT.

The rise of Lower Egypt, its foreign population	58	They are worshipped in fear	61
		Chiun, the foreign Venus	62
The pigmy Pthah	59	Ranpo or Remphan	63
The Cabeiri, or punishing gods	60	The Persian Araita	,,

vi   CONTENTS.

	PAGE		PAGE
The goddess Neith of Sais	63	Egyptian opinions in Palestine, Etruria, Cyprus, Malta, and Sardinia	66
The funereal Papyrus or Ritual	64		
Bigotry and persecution	66		
		The Theory of the Creation	67

THE RELIGION UNDER THE PERSIAN CONQUERORS.

Persian Sun-worship	70	Plato and the School of Heliopolis	71

THE RELIGION UNDER THE PTOLOMIES.

The rise of Alexandria	73	The Apocryphal Books	77
The Greek translation of the Bible by the LXX	75	Philo and the Jewish Monks	79
		The Eleusinian mysteries	80
Its peculiarities	76	The Alexandrian character	81

THE RELIGION UNDER THE ROMANS.

The worship of Serapis	83	Isis and Horus in her arms	85
The worship of Horus	,,	This worship introduced into Rome	86
The trinities	84		
Horus a Child	85		

CHRISTIANITY UNDER THE ROMAN EMPERORS.

Christianity in Egypt	88	Clemens and Origen	97
Its corruption	89	The Trinity of Dionysius	98
It raises the Egyptians	90	The Docetæ	99
Gnosticism; its sculptured gems	91	Christians persecuted as political disturbers	,,
Serpent worship	92	The rebellions against Rome	100
Its Æons, the Ogdoad	93	The worship of Mithra and Manichœism	,,
Its Trinity	95		
The Book of Revelation	96		

CHRISTIANITY UNDER THE BYZANTINE EMPERORS.

The rise of Egyptian opinions and the Arian Controversy	102	Italy and the West adopt the Egyptian opinions	,,
The Council of Nicæa and Athanasius	104	The monastic institutions	110
The Nicene Creed	105	St. Ambrose, St. Augustin, St. Jerome	111
The Athanasian Creed	106		
Temples turned into Churches	107	Theodosius makes Constantinople take Egyptian opinions	112
St. George and the Dragon	109	Egyptian MSS. relics	113

PREFACE.

THE study of error is often only a little less important than the study of truth. The history of the human mind in its progress from ignorance towards knowledge, should tell us the mistakes into which it has sometimes wandered, as well as its steps in the right path. We turn indeed with more pleasure to review the sources from which the world has gained any of its valuable truths, in the hope of there finding some further knowledge which may be equally valuable; while for our errors, so long as we are unwilling to acknowledge them to be errors, we too often shut our eyes, and refuse to be shewn their origin.

The Emperor Marcus Antoninus, in his philosophical work, mentions the several tutors and friends from whom he gained his good habits, and those views of life which he chiefly valued; but though we must suppose that he was aware of some failings in his character, he does not tell us to which of his companions he owed them. And so it is with the benefits of civilization, arts, and religion; and also with the evils of superstition. Modern Europe readily acknowledges how many benefits it received from Rome, from Greece, and from Judea, but has been willing to forget how much of its superstition came from Egypt.

When Christians shall at length acknowledge that many of those doctrines which together now make up orthodoxy, or the religion of the majority, as distinguished from the simple religion which Jesus taught and practised, when they shall acknowledge that many of them are so many sad and lamentable errors, then, and not till then, will they seek to know their origin, and enquire from which of the several branches of Paganism they sprung. They will then see that most of the so called Christian doctrines, that have no place in the New Testament, reached Europe from Egypt, through Alexandria.

The aim of the following pages is not only to explain the Mythology of Egypt, but to show the extraordinary readiness with which its religious opinions were copied by the neighbouring nations, particularly by the Greeks and Romans. In matters of religion, the more ignorant part of those two nations bowed in reverence to the greater earnestness and seriousness of the Egyptians, who were at the same time so remarkably rich in mythological invention. Pagan Greece received from Egypt all that part of its religion which related to a future state of rewards and punishments, and though Christian Greece was for a short time too intelligent to take the whole of the Egyptian mysticism and superstition, yet Christian Rome, from which our own opinions were chiefly learned, had no such hesitation, and was at all times a most willing pupil.

These facts may receive some explanation from two known laws of the human mind. First, among religious persons the fear of doing wrong makes them more afraid of falling into scepticism than into credulity; and those who believe more, whether they believe wisely or unwisely, are apt to think themselves on safer ground than those who believe less. In the case of a proposition in science, when the arguments for it and against it seem equal, the reasoner withholds his assent; but in the case of a religious dogma or article of faith, the mind in its weakness fancies it safer to accept it than to reject it. The reasoning powers are in part overruled by the feelings. In religious controversy, both parties, the believer and the doubter, usually feel that the reproach of disbelief, which it is in the power of one to throw against the other, hits a much harder blow than the reproach of credulity and superstition, which is all that the other can fling back again. It is only among irreligious persons and scoffers that the feelings strengthen the other side, and that disbelief can shut the door against argument by an equally blind and unfair claim to superiority. Hence arises the power which superstitious and complicated systems of religions have of spreading themselves, and hence the weakness of good sense when setting up its simple truths against the encroachments of such many-sided errors.

Secondly, earnestness and sincerity are the most powerful helps by which we enforce our opinions and convert our neighbours. And there was far more real conviction of the truth of their religion among the Egyptians than among their Greek and Roman neighbours. Hence the opinions of the more ignorant lived and spread, while the opinions held with hollowness and insincerity by the more enlightened died away.

The following are the principal doctrines which are most certainly known to be common to Egyptian Mythology and modern orthodoxy, as distinguished from the religion of Jesus. They include the Trinity, the two natures of Christ, and the atonement by vicarious sufferings.

1st. That the creation and government of the world is not the work of one simple and undivided Being, but of one God, made up of several persons. This is the doctrine of Plurality in Unity.

2nd. That happiness or the favour of the Judge of the living and the dead could scarcely be hoped for, either from his justice or his mercy, unless an atoning sacrifice had been paid to him on our behalf, by a divine being; and that mankind, or some part of them, may hope to have their sins forgiven because of the merits and intercession of that Being, and to be excused from punishment because he consented to be sacrificed for them. With the Egyptians there were four such chief mediators.

3rd. That among the gods or persons which compose the godhead, one, though a god, could yet suffer pain and be put to death.

4th. That a god, or man, or being half god and half man, once lived upon earth, who had been born of an earthly mother, but without an earthly father.

It may amuse while it will help our argument to mention also a few of the less important Egyptian opinions which are still common among us. Trifles sometimes declare their origin more certainly than opinions and habits of greater importance, which may be thought common to the human mind. Among the most interesting is the wedding ring. The Egyptian gold, before the introduction of coinage, had been usually kept in the form of a ring; and the Egyptian at his marriage placed one of these pieces of gold on his wife's finger in token of his entrusting her with all his property. The early Christians, says Clemens, saw no harm in following this custom; and in our own marriage ceremony, the man places the same plain ring of gold, on his bride's finger, when he says, "With all my worldly goods I thee endow."

It was one of the duties of the priests of Philæ to

purchase of the river Nile a bountiful overflow by throwing a piece of gold into the stream once a year, and hence probably the Venetians borrowed their custom of Wedding the Adriatic by throwing a gold ring into the sea. At the same time the Doge's cap was copied from the crown of Lower Egypt.

Our Christmas game of drawing lots for the title of King and Queen, is Egyptian. It was called by the Alexandrians the game of Basilinda; and Tacitus mentions the quarrel between Nero and Brittanicus, when they were playing at this game in Rome.

The Egyptian day for eating sugared cakes, had been our twentieth of January, but it was in the fourth century changed to be kept fourteen days earlier; and the sugared cake of the Egyptians now marks the feast of Epiphany, or Twelfth Night.

The feast of candles, which in the time of Herodotus was celebrated at Sais, in honour of the goddess Neith, is yet marked in our almanack as Candlemas Day, or the Purification of the Virgin Mary.

When the Roman Catholic priest shaves the crown of his head, it is because the Egyptian priest had done the same before. When the English clergyman, though he preaches his sermon in a silk or woollen robe, may read the liturgy in no dress but linen, it is because linen was the clothing of the Egyptians. Two thousand years before the bishop of Rome pretended to hold the keys of heaven and earth, there was an Egyptian priest with the high sounding title of Appointed keeper of the two doors of heaven, in the city of Thebes.

Christian art also owes much to the Egyptian imagination. The Virgin Mary rising to heaven, standing upon a crescent moon, very closely resembles Isis as the dog star rising heliacally. (See Fig. 104.) The figure of the Almighty, with head and out-stretched arms at the head of the picture, particularly in the early pictures, when the head hung downwards, is the same in design as that of Horus at the top of many a funeral papyrus (see page 83). The figure of a triangle to represent the Trinity was clearly borrowed from Pagan Egypt (see page 95).

The supposed arts of astrology and witchcraft were more particularly Egyptian; the conjuror's word of Abracadabra is a corruption of the Greek word Abrasax, which is itself a corruption of the Egyptian *hurt me not*, by which they hoped to warn off evil spirits; and fortunetellers are even yet called Egyptians or Gyspies. When Shakespear brings upon the stage the queen of the witches she bears the name of Hecate, one of the well-known names of Isis.

These fanciful customs and foolish opinions and traditions of art, help to show that although the old Egyptian race has ceased to be a nation for more than twelve hundred years, during which its history has been neglected, and its very existence often forgotten, yet the Egyptian mind still has a most important influence upon our modern civilization. Protestant Europe is even now struggling to throw off the graver errors of the Nicene Creed and the Atonement, which Rome received from Egypt fifteen centuries ago.

  Highbury Place,
   June, 1863.

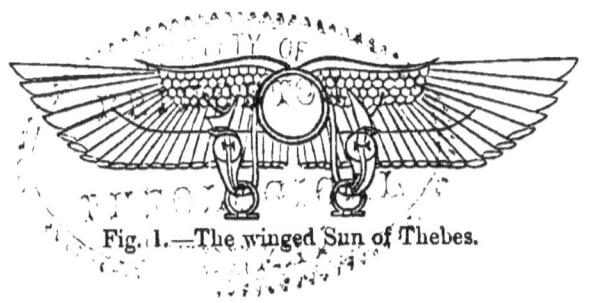

Fig. 1.—The winged Sun of Thebes.

THE EGYPTIAN MYTHOLOGY.

THE history of religious error is the history of the mind wandering in its search after Truth. We meet among the gross idolatry of one nation, as in the purer religion of another nation, the same acknowledgement that man is not his own creator, and that he is dependent for his welfare upon the will of some being or beings more powerful than himself.

The cultivated man, when studying the wonders of the creation around him, traces them back through numerous secondary causes to one great First Cause, and thus arrives at the belief in One Undivided God; and feels more sure of the truth of his reasoning in proportion to the simplicity to which it leads him. On the other hand, an observing but unphilosophical man, in the childhood of the world, when he had noted the various secondary causes which produce all the effects which meet his senses, would perhaps look no further; and he thus arrived at the belief in a variety of gods. But this is not always the case. Some nations seem, like the modern Turks, to have arrived at a belief in one God, as if from indolence of mind, from blind fatalism, from mere want of observation of the numerous causes which are working around them. Thus many of the Arabic races in the neighbourhood of Egypt, as well as the Israelites, traced the hand of one only God, or Great First Cause, in all they enjoyed and all they suffered. But the Egyptians, like the Greeks and Romans, seeing so many causes at work, and not perceiving that they might all be set in motion by One First Cause, thought that every blessing that they received, and every misfortune that befel them, was the work of a different god. They thus peopled the seen and the unseen world beyond with a variety of beings or powers. To these they returned thanks for the blessings that they enjoyed, or more often, as led by a melancholy and less grateful disposition, addressed entreaties that they would withhold their injuries and punishments. The sculptured monuments of the country teach us the figures and sometimes the characters of these imaginary beings, together with the cities and parts of the kingdom in which each was more particularly worshipped.

THE RELIGION OF UPPER EGYPT.

First among these gods of the Egyptians was Ra, *the Sun*, or Amun-Ra, *the Great Sun*, whose warmth ripened their harvests, but whose scorching rays made his power felt as much as an enemy as a friend. His sculptured figure wears a cap ornamented with two tall feathers, and sometimes with the figure of the sun. (See Fig. 2.) He was the King of the Gods. He was more particularly the god of Thebes.

Over the portico of the Theban temple there is usually a ball or sun, ornamented with outstretched wings, representing the all-seeing Providence thus watching over and

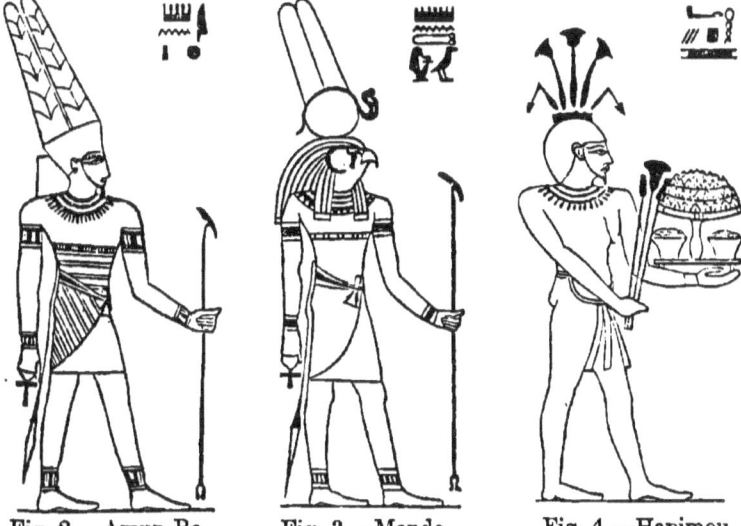

Fig. 2.—Amun-Ra. Fig. 3.—Mando. Fig. 4.—Hapimou.

sheltering the world. From this sun hang two sacred asps wearing the crowns of Upper and Lower Egypt. (See Fig. 1.) Every Egyptian king bore the title of Zera, *the Son of Ra*, and many of the Theban kings took the name of Amunmai, *beloved by Amun*. This god was at times called Adon-Ra, from a word for Lord, known also in the Hebrew language.

In the western half of the Delta, the Sun was worshipped as Mando-Ra. Like Amun-Ra, he wears the two tall feathers, and the Sun on his head, but he differs from him in having a hawk's face. (See Fig. 3.) In our woodcuts these gods each carry in the left hand a staff, with an animal's head, and in the right hand the character for life. A cow's tail, the ornament of royalty, hangs down behind from the waistband. After the fall of the kings of Thebes, we find a violent attempt was made by the kings of the city of Mendes, to introduce into Thebes the worship of Mando-Ra, in place of Amun-Ra.

Next was Hapimou, *the Nile*, whose waters were the chief source of their food, whose overflow marked the limits between the cultivated land and the desert; to him they owed nothing but grateful thanks. He is a figure of both sexes, having the beard of a man and the breasts of a child-bearing woman. (See Fig. 4.) He carries in his arms fruits and flowers, and sometimes waterfowls.

Another great god was their narrow valley, the country in which they lived, clearly divided from the yellow desert by the black Nile-mud, by which it was covered and made fertile, and hence called Chemi, the *Black* Land, or when made into a person, Chem, or Ham. He was the father of their race, called in the Bible, one of the sons of Noah, and considered by themselves the god of increase, the Priapus of the Greeks. Chem has a cap with two tall feathers like that of Amun-Ra, so large that it was necessary to give him a metal support to hold it on the head. His right

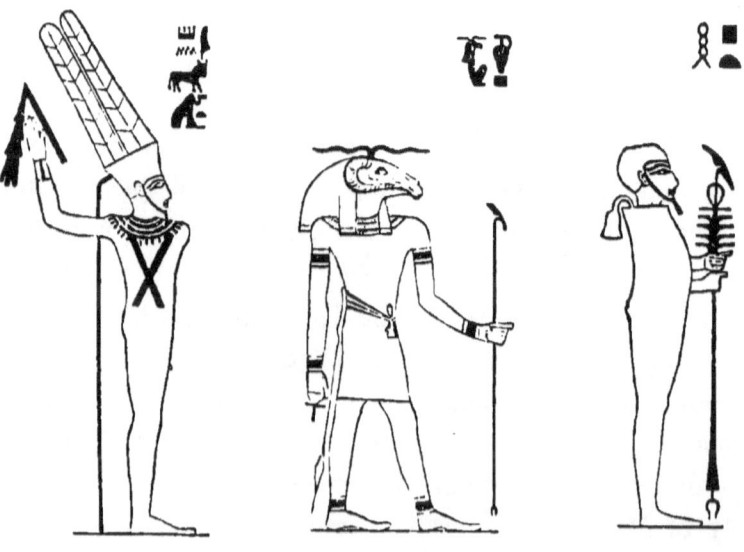

Fig. 5.—Chem.   Fig. 6.—Kneph.   Fig. 7.—Pthah.

arm is raised and holds a whip, his left arm is hid under his dress, which is the tight garment of the Egyptian women. (See Fig. 5.) In consequence of the confusion arising from the Egyptian guttural, his name is in the Hieroglyphics usually spelled THM, as Champsi, *the crocodile*, becomes Tempsi on the eastern side of the Delta.

Kneph, *the Wind* or *Air*, or *Breath* of our bodies, was supposed to be the god of Animal and Spiritual Life. He has the head and horns of a ram. (See Fig. 6.)

Pthah, the god of Fire, was more particularly the god of Memphis, as Amun-Ra of Thebes; and the kings in that city were said to be "Beloved by Pthah." His figure is bandaged like a mummy, and his head shaven like a priest. (See Fig. 7.)

Having thus created for themselves a number of gods, their own feelings, and what they saw around them, would naturally lead them to create an equal number of goddesses. Of these Neith, the Heavens, was one. She is often drawn with wings stretched out as if covering the whole earth. At other times she is formed into an arch, with her feet and fingers on the ground, while her body forms the blue vault overhead, and is spangled with stars. At other times she is simply a woman, with the hieroglyphical character for her name as the ornament on the top of her head. (See Fig. 8.) She was particularly worshipped at Sais, and the kings of that city are styled "Beloved by Neith."

Isis, or Isitis, the Earth, or rather the *corn-bearing Land*, the mother of all creation, was another and perhaps the chief favourite with the nation. Her name is derived from SAT, *to sow seed*, like the Latin Ceres. She is known by the throne upon her head, because a throne forms the first

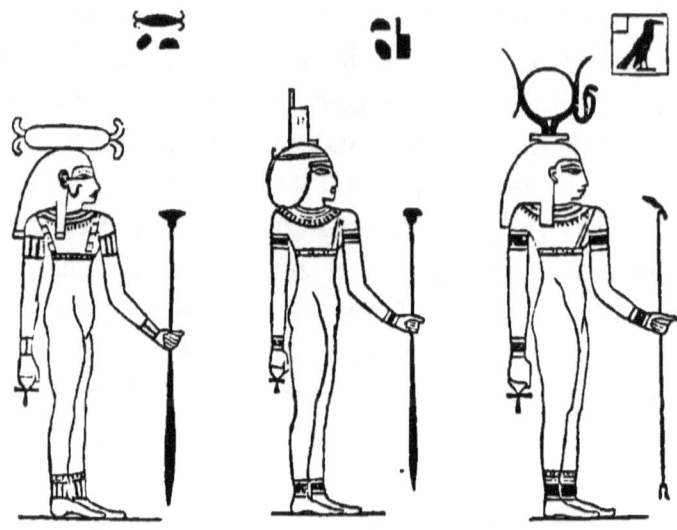

Fig. 8.—Neith.   Fig. 9.—Isis.   Fig. 10.—Athor.

syllable of her name. (See Fig. 9.) But she had so many characters that she is called by the Greeks, the goddess with ten thousand names. She is sometimes Maut, *the mother goddess*, sometimes Hecate, *the sorceress*.

Other goddesses were attributes or feelings made into persons, such as Athor the goddess of Love and Beauty. She has cow's horns, (see Fig. 10,) and sometimes a cow's head. She also is sometimes called Maut, *the mother*. She belonged to Upper Egypt, and was the wife of Amun-Ra, and gave her name to the city of Aphroditopolis.

Pasht, the goddess of Virtue, has a cat's head. See Fig. 11. She belonged to Lower Egypt, and gave her name to the city of Bubastis. Amunothph III., however, of Thebes, particularly styled himself "Beloved by Pasht."

Mo is sometimes the god, sometimes the goddess of Truth and Justice, and is distinguished by ostrich feathers on the head.

When the land was divided into separate estates or properties, Thoth, the *Pillar* or Landmark at the corner of the field, became an important god; and as the owner's name was carved upon it, he was the god of letters and of all learning. He has the head of an ibis, because the ibis perches on the top of the post. He is often in the act of writing, or of counting the years on the notches at the back of a palm branch from which the leaves have been broken off. (See Fig. 12.) This palm branch is the hieroglyphical character for the word "year." Thoth was by the Greeks called Hermes, a name which has the same meaning, *a pillar*. The sacred books of the priests were all supposed to have been written by Thoth.

Fig. 11.—Pasht.

Besides these visible objects and attributes or qualities already described, there was a third class of gods, who were spoken of as if they had once been mortal and had lived upon earth. These were Osiris, the husband of Isis; and their son Horus, so named from Chori, *strong;* and Anubis, their second son; and Nephthys, the sister and companion of Isis; and the wicked Typhon, who put Osiris to death. Osiris, like Pthah, is bandaged as a mummy. He wears a tall mitre with a ball on the top, with or without two feathers as side pieces. He holds two sceptres, one is a whip and one is a crosier. (See Fig. 13.) His name is derived from OSH, *a decree*, and IRI, *to do*, and it means the judge. Horus has a hawk's head, and wears the double

Fig. 12.—Thoth.   Fig. 13.—Osiris.   Fig. 14.—Horus.

crown of Upper and Lower Egypt, formed of a plate of gold over or around the mitre, as described in Exodus xxviii. xxix. (See Fig. 14.) Sometimes he is a crowned hawk. Anubis has the head of a dog or a jackal, (see Fig. 15,) or is represented as the animal a jackal. He never takes a foremost place among the gods, but usually stands as the attendant or servant of Osiris.

Nephthys is known by her name, a dish and a house, upon her head. (See Fig. 16.) It means *Mistress of the house*, or *Lady*. Typhon is a hippopotamus, usually walking on its hind legs, and with female breasts,—(see Fig. 17;) sometimes with sword in his hand, to show his wicked nature. He is the chief author of evil. In Acts xxvii. 14, a tempestuous wind is called a Typhonian wind.

The above list of gods was further increased by copying the arrangements of a family. Thus Pthah, the god of fire, had a son named Imothph, the god of science, or medicine.

Fig. 15.—Anubis.   Fig. 16.—Nephthys.   Fig. 17.—Typhon.

Amun-Ra and his wife Athor had a son named Chonso, who is sometimes only distinguished from his father by the youthful lock of hair on the right side of his head; and sometimes he is known by his having a hawk's face, like Horus, and on his head, not the sun, but the new moon. (See Fig. 18.) To all these numerous gods a father was given in the person of Seb, or Sebek, the crocodile. (See Fig. 19.)

Of these gods Osiris and his family alone had any biography. They once lived upon earth. His wife and

Fig. 18.—Chonso.   Fig. 19.—Seb.

sister Isis was a goddess, while Osiris himself had two natures; he was partly god and partly man. He was put to death by the wicked Typhon, the hippopotamus, and his limbs scattered to the four winds. These Isis collected and put together again, and Osiris returned to life, but not upon earth. He became Judge of the dead in the infernal regions, with the title of Ro-t-Amenti, or *king of hell*, whence the Greeks borrowed the name of Rhadamanthus. His son Horus revenged his father's death, and is styled the Avenger of his father. Horus was the last of the gods that reigned upon earth. Hence he was styled Horus the king. His hawk's head has also the same meaning; the hawk was the bird of royalty. The death of Osiris was piously lamented by Isis and her sister Nephthys; and once a year, the Egyptians joined their priests in a melancholy procession through the streets, singing a doleful ditty called the Maneros, or *Song of Love*, which was to console the goddess for the death of her husband. But this grief for the death of Osiris did not escape some ridicule; for Xenophanes the Ionian wittily remarked to the priests of Memphis, that if they thought Osiris a man they should not worship him, and if they thought him a god they need not talk of his death and sufferings. This story the Greeks copied, and have given us in the form of the loves and lamentations of Venus, a goddess, for Adonis, who was a mortal. The boar which killed Adonis is no other than the hippopotamus Typhon. This shows us how in poetry, as in architecture and sculpture, Greek taste was sometimes willing to make use of Egyptian invention.

Of all the gods Osiris alone had a place of birth and a place of burial. His birthplace was mount Sinai, called by the Egyptians mount Nissa. Hence was derived the god's Greek name Dio-nysus, which is the same as the Hebrew Jehovah-Nissi. This name Moses gave to the Almighty when he set up an altar to Him at the foot of the holy mountain, a spot sacred alike with Jews and Egyptians. See Exodus xvii. 15. Many cities claimed the honour of being the burial place of Osiris, and thence perhaps the profit arising from the offerings to his shrine. The honour, however, seems at last to have been thought to belong more particularly to the island of Philæ.

This story of a dying god shows how little the Egyptians believed him to be an eternal self-existent Being. Indeed, the belief in more than one God is almost a disbelief in any god, in the highest sense of the word; as there can only be one Being who is self-existent, all-powerful, and everywhere present. And the second belief that one out of many gods should die, is hardly more irrational than the first belief that there are many gods. In both cases the believer gives a lower meaning to the word "god" than is given to it by him who worships only one such Being. But our own better views of theology should not lead us to despise these rude beginnings, and first steps in religion, by this earliest of nations.

The belief in One God supposes that the world is being governed by Power acting upon one settled plan, which is shown, by observation, to be both Wise and Good, in a degree so far beyond our understanding, that we may safely think it infinite. A belief in more Gods than one supposes that the world is governed by power acting with an occasional change of plan, which if sometimes wise and good is by no means always so. And a belief in the numerous gods above described, shows that the Egyptians thought too much of the trials and misfortunes, and too little of the blessings that befall us, and fancied that the ways of Providence were so irregular, and so much less wise and good than if governed by one of themselves, that they could only be explained by supposing a crowd of unseen beings, of whom sometimes one and sometimes another took the trouble to meddle with the doings of men. Such was the unhappy theology of Egypt.

The long list of gods mentioned above was again further increased in two ways. The priests sometimes made a new god by uniting two or three, or four into one, and at other times by dividing one into two or three, or more. Thus out of Horus and Ra they made Horus-Ra, called by the Greeks Aroeris. Out of Osiris and Apis the bull of Memphis, the priests of Memphis made Osiri-Apis or Serapis. He carries the two sceptres of Osiris, and has a bull's head. (See Fig. 20.) Out of Amun-Ra and Ehe the bull of Heliopolis, the priests of the East of the Delta made Amun-Ra-Ehe. To this again they added a fourth character, that of Chem, and made a god Amun-Ra-Ehe-Chem. Out of Kneph *the Spirit*, and Ra *the Sun*, they made Kneph-Ra. Out of Sebek and Ra, they made Sebek-Ra. In this way the Egyptians worshipped a plurality in Unity.

Fig. 20.—Serapis.

In the case of division they had two of the name of Anubis, one for Upper Egypt and one for Lower Egypt, and afterwards as many as six of that name. They divided

THE TRINITIES. 13

Horus into three persons upon the rule that everything perfect has three parts; and in addition to Horus the king the son of Isis, and Horus-Ra before mentioned, they made a third, Horus the Scarabeus or beetle. While making out of the god Osiris, the new person Osiri-Apis or Serapis, they made a second by uniting him to Pthah in the person of Pthah-sokar-Osiris.

The gods were very much grouped in sets of three, and each city had its own trinity. In Thebes it was Amun-Ra, Athor, and Chonso, or father, mother, and son. (See Fig. 21.) Sometimes, however, they were arranged as father, son, and mother, placing Chonso between his two parents. In Abousimbel and Derr in Nubia, the trinity is Pthah,

Fig. 21.—Amun-Ra, Maut, and Chonso.

Amun-Ra, and Horus-Ra, and these are the three gods to whom Rameses II. is sacrificing the Philistines, in the sculptures at Beyroot. At Abousimbel the king also worships Amun-Ra, Horus-Ra, and Horus of Lower Egypt. At Wady Seboua he is seated in a group with Pthah, Kneph, and Athor. At Silsilis he worships Amun-Ra, Horus-Ra, and Hapimou, the Nile. At Philæ the trinity is Osiris, Isis, and Horus, a group indeed common to most parts of Egypt. Other groups were Isis, Nephthys, and Horus, (See Fig. 22); or Isis, Nephthis, and Osiris; and with a national love for mysticism the priests often declared

Fig. 22.

that the three in some undescribed way only made one person. The above figures indeed do not declare that the three gods are only one; but we have a hieroglyphical inscription in the British Museum as early as the reign of Sevechus of the eighth century before the Christian Era, showing that the doctrine of Trinity in Unity already formed part of their religion, and stating that in each of the two groups last mentioned the three gods only made one person. (Egypt. Inscript., pl. 36, 4, 5.)

The sculptured figures on the lid of the sarcophagus of Rameses III., now at Cambridge, show us the king not only as one of a group of three gods, but also as a Trinity in Unity in his own person. He stands between the goddesses Isis and Nephthys, who embrace him as if he were the lost Osiris, whom they have now found again. (See Fig. 23.) We further know him to be in the character of Osiris by the two sceptres which he holds in his hands; but at the same time the horns upon his head are those of the goddess Athor, and the ball and feathers above are the ornaments of the god Ra. Thus he is at once Osiris, Athor, and Ra.

After the gods the useful and hurtful animals next received worship, the first in acknowledgement of their services, and the latter that they might withhold their injuries. The ox was worshipped

Fig. 23.

because it ploughed the field; and it was never slain because its flesh was very little wanted for food in the warm climate of Egypt, and where they had the buffalo for food, which will not consent to plough in the furrow. See Job xxxix. 10. The sacred bull was called Apis in Memphis and the west of the Delta, and Amun-ehe, or as the Greeks wrote it Mnevis, in Heliopolis and the east of the Delta. He was ornamented with the figure of the sun or full moon between his horns. (See Fig. 24.) The crocodile was worshipped because he was the terror of those who approached the river's bank. He was called Seb, and made the father of all the gods, and the patron god of some of the Ethiopian Kings. Selk, *the scorpion*, was a tortur-

Fig. 24.—Apis.

THE SACRED ANIMALS.

ing goddess, perhaps Isis in one of her numerous forms. The Ibis was valued because it destroyed the crocodile's eggs, the cat because it was the enemy of vermin; and the dog and jackal were valued for their service as scavengers. The venomous snakes, and those that were not venomous, were alike honoured, the first as gods of evil, and the second as gods, or rather goddesses, of good. (See Fig. 25.) The hawk was a bird of dignity, and so dedicated to Horus the king. The Scarabæus or beetle rolls up before it a ball of dirt in which it wraps its eggs, and hence was made sacred to the Sun. (See Fig. 26.)

Fig. 25.

These animals were looked upon as the representatives of the gods mentioned above, and each received a more particular honour in its own city where their embalmed remains were in many cases buried with almost royal honour. In many cities the earnestness and zeal for their favourite animal often carried the Egyptians into civil war. Juvenal mentions the war in his time between the city of Ombos, where the crocodile was worshipped, and the city of Tentyra, whose people were celebrated for their skill in catching and killing those fierce animals. The Emperor Hadrian was called into Egypt by a rising yet more serious, which might have led to a war between the eastern and the western half of the Delta, as to whether a bull was to be an Apis or a Mnevis. Diodorus the historian was present when the mob rose against the Roman guards because a soldier had killed a cat. The city of Thebes alone had no sacred animals; hence as Memphis was the second city in size, Apis the bull of

Fig. 26.

WORSHIP OF FOREFATHERS.

Memphis was the animal most thought of by the nation at large. The sums of money spent upon its funeral were enormous; and it was embalmed and buried in a granite sarcophagus with royal honours in the caverns tunnelled into the hill on the west side of the city. No national festival was of equal importance with the ceremony of leading the new Apis into its temple in Memphis, when an animal had been found marked with the right spots. The priests told Herodotus that its birth was miraculous, that it had no earthly father, but was engendered by divine influence, and that the cow, its mother, never had a second calf.

From a pious regard to those that gave them birth, the Egyptians paid some kind of inferior worship to their father and mother when dead, and to all their forefathers. They dutifully set out food for the use of these dead relations in the neighbourhood of the tombs; and their doing so was carefully mentioned on their own funeral tablets as an act which, like the worship of the gods, they had not neglected in their lifetime. The sculpture which shows the dead man on his knees presenting his offerings to the gods, shows him standing to present the same offerings to his ancestors. When he brings fire and water to the one he does the same to the others. Such food would soon be devoured by the beasts and birds of the desert; and in the inscriptions Anubis the jackal is called, The devourer of what is set out for the dead. The Egyptian superstitions are usually forbidden in the Mosaic Law, and in Deut. xxvi. 13, 14, we see that the Israelites were forbidden to set apart any food for the dead.

Every king of Egypt, even while living, was added to

the number of the gods, and declared to be the Son of Ra, which was the title set over the second oval of his name. (See Fig. 27.) He was then sometimes made into the third person of a Trinity, in which case he took the place of the god Chonso, in Fig. 21. He denied that he owed his birth to the father from whom he inherited the crown; he claimed to be born, like the bull Apis, by a miraculous conception. He styled his mother the wife of Amun-Ra, which explains the mistake of Diodorus Siculus who calls the tombs of the queens near Thebes, the tombs of Jupiter's concubines. Many of the more favourite kings after their death continued to receive the same divine worship.

Fig. 27.

This opinion of the miraculous birth of the kings is well explained in a series of sculptures on the wall of the temple of Luxor. (See Fig. 28.) First, the god Thoth, with the head of an ibis, and with his ink and pen-case in his left hand, as the messenger of the gods, like the Mercury of the Greeks, tells the maiden queen Mautmes, that she is to give birth to a son, who is to be king Amunothph III. Secondly, the god Kneph, *the spirit*, with a ram's head, and the goddess Athor, with the sun and cow's horns upon her head, both take hold of the queen by her hands, and put into her mouth the character for life, which is to be the life of the coming child. Thirdly, the queen, when the child is to be born, is seated on the midwife's stool, as described in Exodus i. 16; two of the attending nurses rub her hands to ease the pains of child-birth, while another of the nurses holds up the baby, over which is written the name of king Amunothph III. He holds his finger to his mouth to mark his infancy;

he has not yet learned to speak. Lastly, the several gods or priests attend in adoration upon their knees to present their gifts to this wonderful child, who is seated in the midst of them and is receiving their homage. In this picture we have the Annunciation, the Conception, the Birth, and the Adoration, as described in the First and Second Chapters of Luke's Gospel; and as we have historical assurance that the chapters in Matthew's Gospel which contain the Miraculous Birth of Jesus are an after addition not in the earliest manuscripts, it seems probable that these two poetical chapters in Luke may also be unhistorical, and be borrowed from the Egyptian accounts of the miraculous birth of their kings.

The Egyptians had a sacred tree, but want of

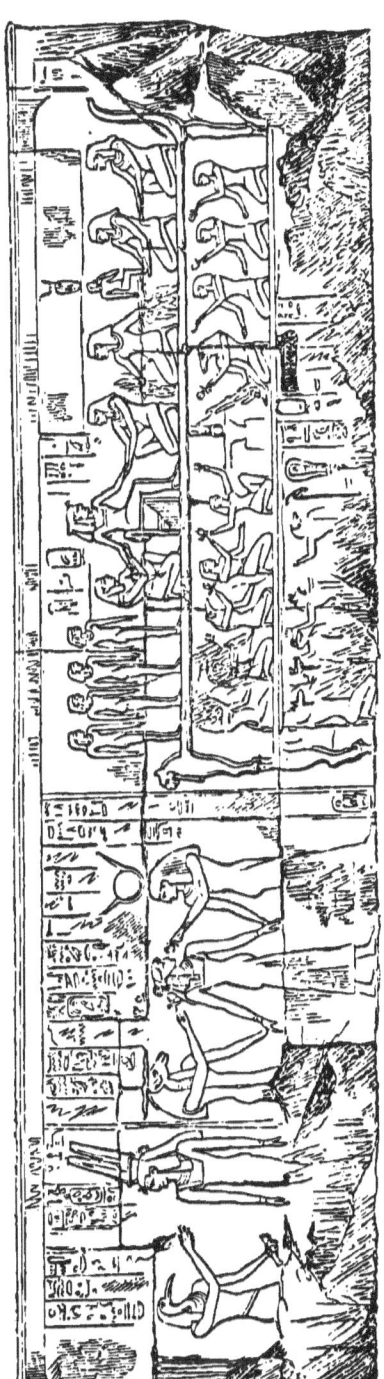

Fig. 28.—The Birth of King Amunothph III.

exactness in the accounts of it leads us to doubt whether it was an Acasia of the sensitive class, that bowed its leaves in silent hospitality to the weary traveller that sat under its slender shade, or whether it was a fruit-bearing tree the *Balanites Ægyptiaca*. The goddess Neith seated in its branches sometimes is pouring out the characters for life and power on the head of the king. When the pretended philosopher Apollonius of Tyana visited Thebes, the tree in a womanly voice declared him to be a teacher sent from heaven. In this it may be compared to the bush out of which the voice spoke to Moses, in Exodus iii. 2. But at other times it is more like the tree of life, or that of knowledge, in the garden of Eden in Genesis iii. as when a priest, after death, is painted as kneeling before the tree, and his soul stands beside him in form of a bird with human head; and they are both drinking the water which the goddess is pouring into their mouths. (See Fig. 29.)

Fig. 29.

The Egyptians of course worshipped the statues of their gods as the representations of the gods themselves who were unseen. But with what religious feelings they worshipped the animals and the kings must be doubtful. In England no sportsman shoots a robin redbreast. In Holland nobody would hurt a stork. Confucius orders the Chinese not to hurt the ox which ploughs the fields for them. The Israelites were ordered not to destroy a fruit tree, even if it belonged to an enemy. (Deut. xx. 19.) No Dutch child would be so wicked as to pluck up the rush which grows on the bank of the canal, and holds it together by its roots. From feelings such as these may have grown the religious reverence of the Egyptians for animals and plants. So on the other hand the shudder felt at the sight of a lion, of a venomous serpent, and even, by some persons, of a spider, may have led to feelings akin to those with which men have worshipped a devil or a god to be feared, and have hoped to appease him by gifts.

Fig. 30.

As to their kings, they were at the head of the priesthood, and received religious respect accordingly. It was part of their duty to present the offerings at the altar of the temple, not only on their own behalf, but on behalf of the nation, to buy the favour of the gods or turn aside their anger. On the walls and columns of the temple, the most common sculpture is the group of the king presenting his gift to the god as an atonement for his own sins and the sins of the people. (See Fig. 30.) They were mediators between their subjects and the gods. We have a Greek inscription from Egypt declaring that Alexander the Great, being a god, is able to appease Olympic Jove.

The Egyptians were of a gloomy serious disposition, and they worshipped in fear rather than in gratitude. Their prayers and sacrifices were sin-offerings rather than thank-offerings. The architecture of their temples was in harmony with their religion. The inner sanctuary, the holy of holies, was always a dark room. Fig. 31 is the ground plan of the temple of Errebek in Thebes, built by Oimenepthah I., and finished by his son Rameses II. The worshippers were allowed to enter a first courtyard, and a second courtyard through gateways formed of massive towers. An avenue between two rows of sphinxes brought them to the portico, under which the sacrifices and libations were made in their sight and on their behalf. But none but the priests ever entered the small dark rooms beyond. The portico was handsome but heavy, and grand rather than beautiful; the flat roof was upheld by a row of strong closely set columns. (See Fig. 32.)

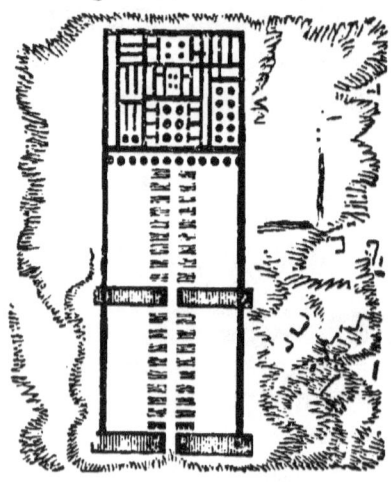

Fig. 31.—Temple of Errebek.

But if we would know the styles of the yet earlier Egyptian temples, we must seek for models of them not in Egypt, but in Ethiopia and in the peninsula of Sinai; as fashions change faster near the capital, and the older style of art must be looked for at a distance. Fig. 33 is the plan of the temple of Seboua in Ethiopia, half way between the first and the second cataract. It was built in the reign of Rameses II., but as it is at a distance from Thebes it may be supposed to show us what the Theban temples were some centuries earlier. Here the more sacred rooms are caves in the side of the hill, while the grand hall, the large courtyard.and the avenue of sphinxes by which it is approached, are on the plain in front of the hill.

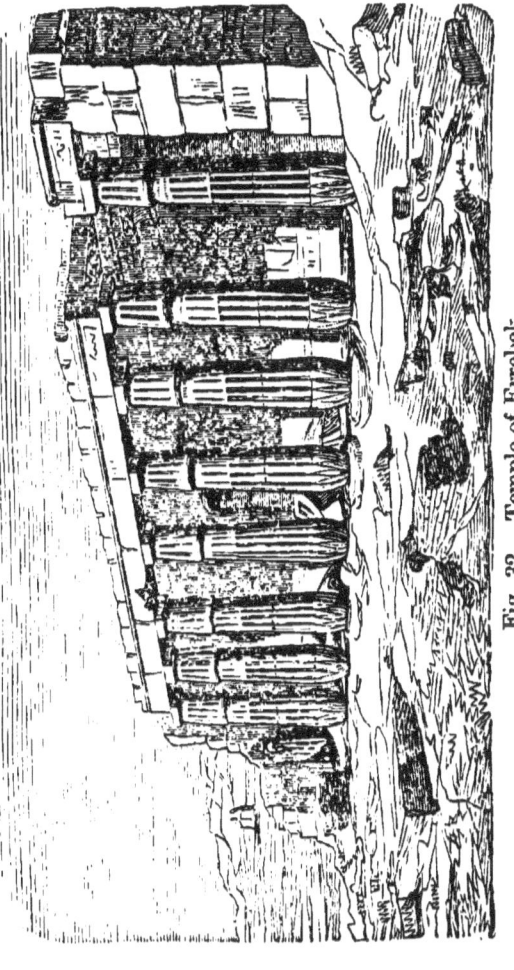

Fig. 32.—Temple of Errebek.

The yet larger temple of Abousimbel is wholly tunnelled into the hill, and there the sun Amun-Ra was worshipped in chambers ornamented with painted sculptures upon which his rays never fell. The small temple of Sarbout el Kadem, near mount Sinai, explains very satisfactorily the progress of temple architecture among the Egyptians. (See Fig. 34.) Here the inner sanctuary is of one date, a

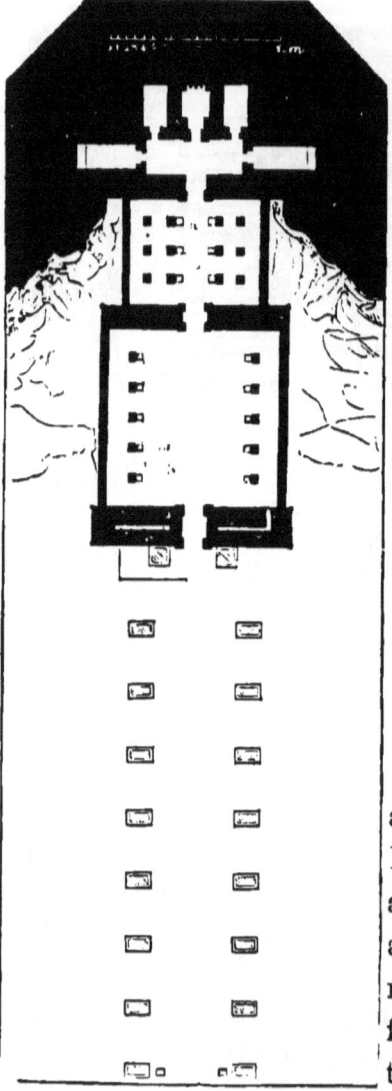

Fig. 33.—Temple of Seboua.

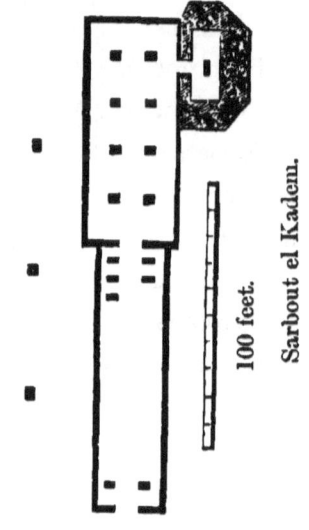

Fig. 34.

cave in the side of the hill, formed by king Amunmai Thori III.; while the hall and courtyard belonging to it, and in the open air, were added by Thothmosis II. and III., two hundred years afterwards. The inner, older, and darker room, very naturally formed the Sanctuary for the more modern temple that was added to it.

In all the temples of which any ruins remain, built later than that of Errebek, we note a change in the portico, which marks an altered state of the religious or rather the ecclesiastical feelings of the people. The portico of the Memnonium built by

Rameses II., and that at Medinet Habou, built by Rameses III., were not open to the eyes of the people in the courtyard like that at Errebek. These newer temples had a low wall running from column to column, which shut out the public from seeing what took place within. The laity were left to imagine the solemnities which their fathers had been allowed to gaze at. This is well shown in the ruined temple of Contra-Latopolis, which was built under the later Ptolemies. See Fig. 35. It is still better shown

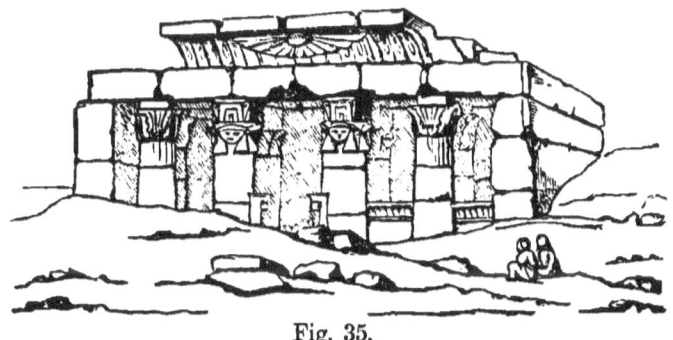

Fig. 35.

in Fig. 36, a restoration of the Temple of Dendera, which though built in even more modern days under the Roman Emperors, yet in this respect is the same as the temples of

Fig. 36.

Rameses II. and III. This low intercolumnar wall, like the screen in our cathedrals between the choir and the nave, betrays a wish on the part of the priests to increase the distance between themselves and the laity. They thus said to the rest of the nation, Stand apart by yourselves, come not near to us, for we are holier than you are. It was after seeing the evils which thus grew out of an established priesthood that the Jewish lawgiver told the Israelites, that they were themselves " a holy nation and a kingdom of priests." Exodus xix. 6. They needed no such separate class; and it would seem that it did not exist in Judea, till after the establishment of the monarchy.

The Egyptian priesthood was hereditary and formed one of the three classes into which the nation was divided, namely the priests, the soldiers, and the cultivators of the soil. They held their estates free from the land tax or rent of one fifth of the crop, as mentioned in Gen. xlvii. 26. They were the only learned or educated people in the kingdom, and consequently they filled every post and office which needed any education. Not only every clergyman, sexton, and undertaker, but every physician and druggist; every lawyer, writing-clerk, schoolmaster, and author; every sculptor, painter, and land-measurer; every conjuror, ventriloquist, and fortune-teller, belonged to the priestly order. Even those posts in the army which required an education, such as secretaryships and clerkships, were held by priests. Much of the skilled labour of the country was under their control. The linen manufactories in the Delta, and the stone quarries between the first and second cataracts, were both managed by the priests.

Every temple had its own hereditary family of priests, who were at the same time magistrates of the city and district, holding their power by the same right as the king held his; and as the king was at the head of the priesthood, the union between church and state was complete. To each of the temples was attached a large body of priests of lower rank, who assisted at the ceremonies and waited on their superiors. The temple of the Memnonium of Thebes is surrounded at the back and at the two sides by vaults

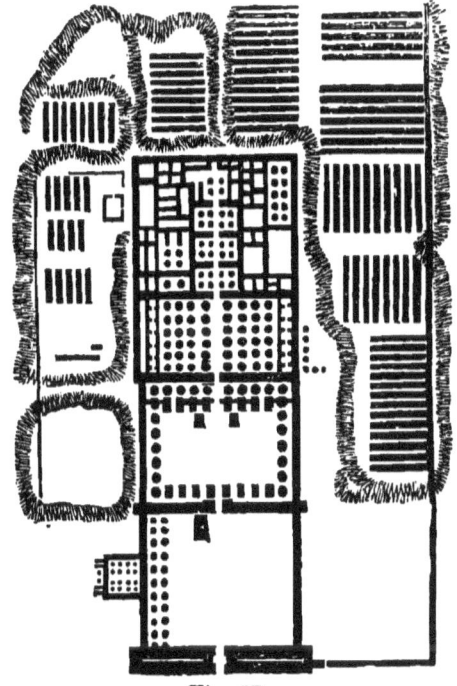

Fig. 37.

built of unburnt brick, which would seem to be each a dwelling for one of the priests of lower rank. These cells were at least 130 in number. See Fig. 37. A smaller number of priests of higher rank, perhaps twenty or fewer, may have lived within the temple, in the small rooms around the sanctuary. The duty of these one or two hundred men, who were maintained at the public expense, was to make sacrifices and offer prayers on behalf of the nation, in gratitude for blessings received, and also in order to appease the gods, whom they feared as much as loved. In the temple on the Island of Philæ, built under the Ptolemies, the priests lived in cells within the two courtyards. Those of lower rank may have had the twelve smaller cells on one side of the inner courtyard, while the chief priest may have dwelt in the larger rooms on the opposite side of this courtyard. (See Fig. 38.) When

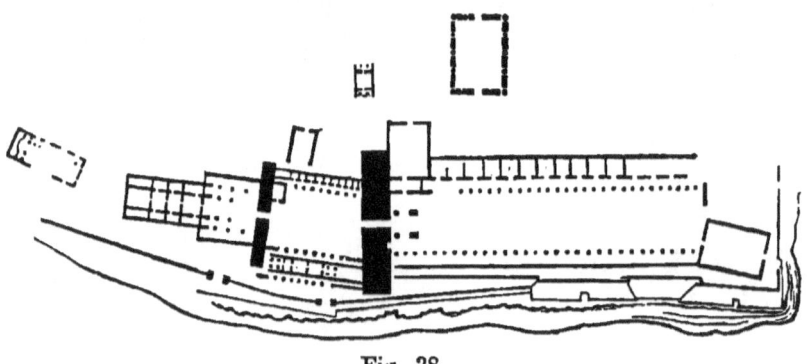

Fig. 38.

the outer courtyard was added to the same temple, fifteen more rather larger cells were built within it for the priests' dwellings. Thus while the cells for the priests belonging to the Memnonium in the middle of the city of Thebes, were outside the walls of the temple, in this temple at Philæ, situated at the frontier of the kingdom, the cells were more cautiously placed within the walls of the fortified building. This temple was one of the places in which Osiris was said to be buried (Diod. Sic. lib. i., 22), and here the priests every day made use of 360 sacred vessels, as they poured out 360 libations of milk in his honour and in token of their grief for his sufferings. No oath was so binding as that sworn in the name of

ORDERS OF PRIESTHOOD.

Him that lies buried at Philæ, and none but priests were allowed to set foot upon this sacred island.

From the sculptures on the sarcophagus of Amyrtæus we learn that the priesthood was divided into four orders, the Soteno, the Othphto, the Nouto, and the Bachano. Of these the Soteno were the chief, as their name implies. The magistrate of the city was a Soten, or as Herodotus writes it, a Sethon. The Nouto, whose name means *Holy*, we may suppose were those who performed the sacrifices and other religious duties of a clergyman. Among the Greeks and Romans, while the priest performed the sacrifices, the philosopher wrote on duties and was the consoler of the afflicted, and the poet wrote on theology with the lives and actions of the gods. But in Egypt, as with ourselves, the priest took the three duties upon himself, and hence he ruled the minds of his hearers with a power wholly unknown in Greece or Rome. The Othphto, whose name means *Dedicated*, were probably those under monastic vows, who were confined within the temple walls and only allowed to speak to strangers through a window. The statues of men seated on the ground in religious idleness, with the chin resting on the knees, probably belong to priests of this class. (See Fig. 39.) The Bachano were the hired servants.

Fig. 39.

How early in the history of Egypt any of the priests were forbidden to marry does not certainly appear; it is only at a rather late time that we find proof that celibacy was thought a religious virtue. But those who lived confined within the cells in the temples were probably at all times unmarried.

Chæremon tells us of the painful self-denial practised by some classes of the Egyptian priests, in their food and clothing and way of life. They often fasted from animal food, and at all times refused many meats as unclean. They prayed thrice a day and passed their time for the most part alone, in study or in religious meditation. They never met one another but at set times, and were seldom seen by strangers. They slept on a hard bed of palm branches, with a still harder wooden and even stone pillow for the head. Small models of this pillow are often found buried with the mummies as proof of the self-denial practised. (See Fig. 43.) These were the steps taken by one class of the priests to gain a power over the minds of their laity. Their more zealous followers practised the same self-torture, and even gashed their bodies with knives in token of grief for their sins, and their full sense of unworthiness.

The Soteno, and the Nouto wore crowns, which were distinguished as belonging one to Upper Egypt and the other to Lower Egypt. The Soteno wore the mitre or tall cap with the ball on the top; this was made of linen, and was the crown of Upper Egypt. (See Fig. 40.) It is that at all times worn by Osiris. (See Fig. 13.) The Nouto wore a flat ring or plate of gold, with a tall piece before and behind.

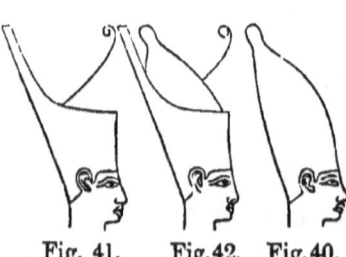

Fig. 41.   Fig. 42.   Fig. 40.

(See Fig. 41.) This was the crown of Lower Egypt.

These two priestly crowns when worn one over the other, form the double crown of Upper and Lower Egypt. (See Fig. 42.) This is the crown of the god Horus. (See Fig. 14.) He was called Horus the king. It was also the usual crown of the King of Egypt, who bore the double priestly title, perhaps pronounced Sot-Nout, meaning *chief* and *holy,* because he was the head of both those orders of priesthood. Both the above-mentioned crowns, the one of linen and the other of gold, were copied by the Israelites and worn the one over the other by the Jewish high priest in the service of the temple. (See Exodus xxviii., 36, 39 ; Leviticus viii., 9.)

Other priestly ornaments, borrowed by the Israelites from Egypt, were the little bells and pomegranates which were sewn on to the hem of the high priest's robe. (See Exodus xxviii., 33.) Many of these golden trinkets are to be found in our Museums among the Egyptian Antiquities, and they seem to have been copied from the painted borders which form the collars round the neck of the wooden mummy cases, and which are made of lotus flower and fruit alternately. (See Fig. 44). The

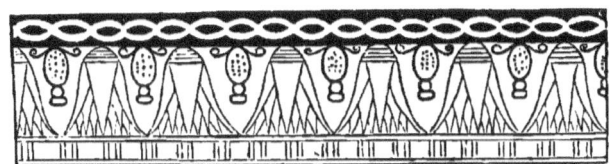

Fig. 44.

Urim and Thummim also, the emblems of *royalty* and *truth,* were borrowed from Egypt, as we learn from their names, which are derived from the Egyptian words OURO, *King,* and THMEI, *justice* or *truth.* In Fig. 45 the god Horus-Ra is Ouro, and the goddess with the feather on her head is Thmei. In Fig. 46, the Uræus or sacred asp is Ouro, and the vulture is Mo, or with feminine article Thmo; and the two together are perhaps a variety of the former ornament. Again Fig. 47

Fig. 45.   Fig. 46.   Fig. 47.

is the goddess Mo, Mei, or Thmei alone. The ark which was borne along by poles resting upon men's shoulders, and contained some of the more sacred emblems of the Jewish religion, need not have been copied from any foreign form of temple service, because it was naturally wanted, when the tabernacle, the centre of their national worship, was moved about from town to town as in the time of the Judges; but we may remark that in a sculpture representing Rameses III. accompanied by his priests and high officers and the sacred bull Apis, we see that an ark of the same size as the Jewish ark, was carried along upon men's shoulders in the sacred procession. (See Fig. 48.)

Fig. 48.

That this Egyptian ark was a prison may be judged from the models of trees at the top; as in some paintings we see wicked imps, the punishing gods, imprisoned in cells which are shown to be pits under ground by the trees growing over them. In Genesis, chap. xxxvii., we read that Joseph was imprisoned by his brothers in a pit or dry well. But what was shut up in the Egyptian ark we are not told, and it is perhaps idle to conjecture; but the only other portable prison or cage that we know of was the basket in later times carried by the priestesses in procession through the streets of Alexandria, which seems to have held a live serpent, the emblem of sin and evil, and the great enemy of the human race. The quarrel between mankind and the great serpent is the subject of many of the sculptures in the tombs, and it always ends with the enemy being conquered and usually taken prisoner, though sometimes killed.

Clemens of Alexandria describes the employments of some of the priests when he tells us which parts of the books of Thoth each undertook to learn and to repeat by heart. The Singer who walked first in the sacred processions bearing the symbols of music, could repeat the books of hymns and the rules for the king's life. The Soothsayer who followed, carrying an hour glass, and a palm branch the emblem of the year, could repeat the four astrological books : one on the moon's phases, one on the fixed stars, and two on their heliacal risings. The Scribe who walked next, carrying a book and the flat rule which held the ink and pen, was acquainted with the geography of the world and of the Nile, and with those books which describe the motions of the sun, moon, and planets, and the furniture of the temple and consecrated places. The Master of the Robes carried the rod of justice, and the sacrificial vase. He understood the ten books relating to education, to the marks on the sacred heifers, and to the worship of the gods, embracing the sacrifices, the first-fruits, the hymns, the prayers, the processions, and festivals. The prophet or preacher who walked last, carrying in his arms the great waterpot, was the president of the temple, and learned in the ten books, called hieratic, relating to the laws, the gods, the management of the temples, and the revenue. Thus of the forty-two chief books of Thoth, thirty-six were learned by these priests, while the remaining six, on the body, its diseases, and medicines, were learned by Pastophori, priests who carried the image of the god in a small shrine. Of these priests we know several from the sculptures and their statues. On a bas-relief in Rome, the Singer carrying the symbols of music is not a priest but a priestess. (See Fig. 49.) Before her walks the Prophet, carrying the great water-pot. (See Fig. 50.) Before him walks the Scribe, carrying his book which is a roll of papyrus. (See Fig. 51.) He has feathers

Fig. 49.—The Singer. Fig. 50.—The Prophet. Fig. 51.—The Scribe. Fig. 52.

in his cap, and in the Rosetta Stone is called a Pterophoros, or *wing bearer*. Among the modern sculptures on the temple of Dendera, we have the soothsayer carrying the hour-glass, which was not invented till long after the fall of Thebes. (See Fig. 53.) And on the sarcophagus of Amyrteus we have a procession of priests each carrying a palm branch (see Egypt. Inscript. Pl. 28 and 30,) accompanying the priests with feathers on their heads. We have also many statues of the scribes, seated on the ground cross-legged with the roll of papyrus on the knees. Statues also of the Pastophori, or shrine-bearers are not uncommon. They are sometimes sitting on the ground and sometimes kneeling.

Fig. 53.

(See Fig. 54.) The shrine or model of a temple usually has in front of it a small figure of the god to whom it is dedicated.

One important office of the priests, was to take out the statues of the gods on certain days of the year, in barges on the Nile. (See Fig. 55). The chief boat carried the statue of Ra and the other principal gods, it was accompanied by other boats containing gods of lower rank. Horus acts as steersman to the boat of Ra. It was part of the enactment by the priests in honour of King Ptolemy Epi-

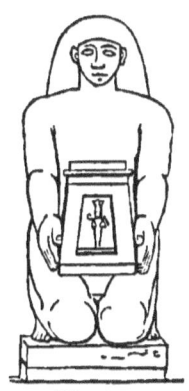

Fig. 54.

THE STANDARDS.

Fig. 55.

phanes, that when the statues of the gods were carried out in this sacred procession, the statue of the king should be carried out with them. The gods on this voyage, were supposed to be going to visit the righteous Ethiopians, who were also, as we learn from Homer, visited by the Greek gods; and Iamblicus tells us that any man who

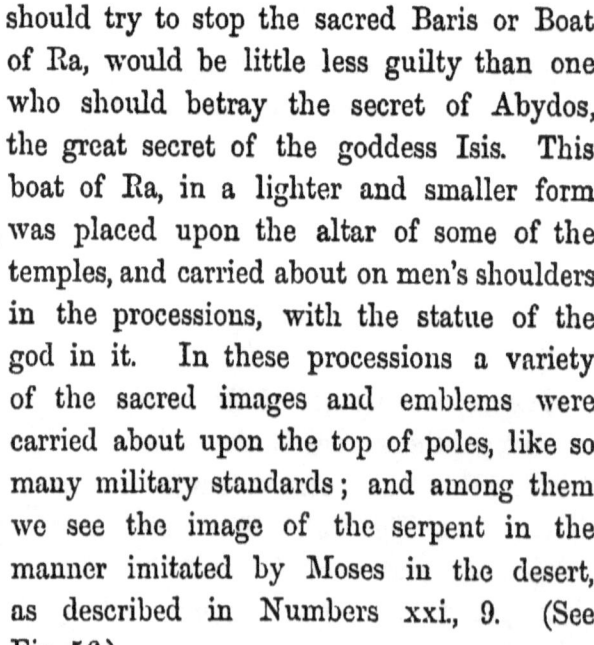

Fig. 56.

should try to stop the sacred Baris or Boat of Ra, would be little less guilty than one who should betray the secret of Abydos, the great secret of the goddess Isis. This boat of Ra, in a lighter and smaller form was placed upon the altar of some of the temples, and carried about on men's shoulders in the processions, with the statue of the god in it. In these processions a variety of the sacred images and emblems were carried about upon the top of poles, like so many military standards; and among them we see the image of the serpent in the manner imitated by Moses in the desert, as described in Numbers xxi., 9. (See Fig. 56.)

Many were the tricks used by the priests to gain a power over the minds of their followers and to strengthen the belief in their holiness. By means of one of these the colossal statue of Amunothph III., seated in the plain of Thebes, uttered its musical notes every morning at sunrise, when the sun's rays first touched its lips. The Septuagint tells us that ventriloquism, or the art of speaking without moving the lips, was also employed to make the bystanders fancy that a statue, or altar, or animal, spoke to them. They could also take up a small serpent, and by pressing the thumb on the nape of the neck throw it into a catalepsy and make it stiff like a rod. In this state they threw it on the ground; and when after a time it regained its power of motion, they said that they had changed a rod into a serpent. This trick was performed by the priests in the presence of Moses (see Exodus vii., 11.) They interpreted dreams and foretold future events by means of a divining cup which had a variety of superstitious figures engraved within it.

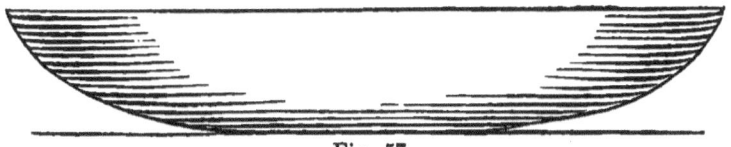

Fig. 57.

We have in the British Museum an Assyrian copy of one of these Egyptian divining cups. (See Fig. 57.) Such may have been the cup with which Joseph divined as mentioned in Genesis xliv., 5. In one temple there was a small window in the roof through which light could be let into a room otherwise dark; and at the proper minute this window was opened, and the sun's rays were allowed to enter and fall upon the face of the god's statue within.

The greater number of the priests were certainly married, and on the funereal tablets, we find a man boasting of his descent through a line of priestesses, perhaps as often as through a line of priests. In the case of the married priests, their wives were priestesses, and their children belonged to the same sacred order afterwards. The priestesses were more particularly musicians to the temple service. Their favourite instrument was a systrum, a bronze ring, with a handle, and pierced with six holes, through which were passed three bronze wires which made a jingling noise when it was shaken. The dress of the priests and priestesses was for the most part the same as that of the laity. The priestesses wore one thin robe, reaching from the neck to the ankles, sometimes loose, but sometimes so tight that they could only take short steps in walking. The priests also wore a thin garment reaching from the shoulders to the knees, and beneath it a short apron round the loins. These were all made of linen, as indeed were the garments of every man in the country. Flax was a native of Egypt, and hence curiously arose the opinion of the neighbouring nations that linen was the clothing most suited for the priesthood. Some few however of the priests are represented as wearing for their clothing the spotted skin of a leopard, with the claws and tail not removed from it. (See Fig. 58.) The monuments show us some priests

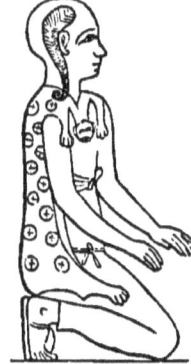

Fig. 58.

with the head wholly shaven, and we see in Genesis xli., 14, that Joseph thought it necessary to shave himself when he went before Pharaoh in the priestly character of interpreter of dreams. In a painting on stucco in the British Museum, a priest has left a small line of hair round the shaven crown of his head, after the fashion of the tonsure, since followed by the Roman Catholics. In our Fig. 58, the priest has the single lock of hair hanging on one side of his head, which at one time was worn only by the kings' sons, and upon the statues of the youthful gods Horus and Chonso; but afterwards it became more common.

The offerings set out upon the altars for gods and ancestors, were for the most part the articles of food which were eaten by the living; such as, the head of a calf, the leg of a stag, a craw-fish, a loaf of bread, and various vegetables. At other times it was a cone of baked clay with a religious sentence

Fig. 59.—Small Votive Pyramid.

stamped on the base, or a small stone pyramid with an

inscription on each of the four sides. (See Fig. 59.) These were used as figurative of any gift, in consequence of the close resemblance of the words TEI, *a gift*, and TAU, *a hill*. On some occasions the priest presented fire and water to the statues of the gods as being the two purest of the elements. The water, or occasionally wine, was poured out of a tall slender jar, while a small quantity of burning charcoal was held forward in a metal ladle with a long handle to it, (see Fig. 60), where we have figures of the king, the queen, and their son attending upon two priests, who are making the offerings. We learn from Jeremiah xliv., 18, that this charcoal fire was used to burn incense, as the Jews when living in Egypt are described

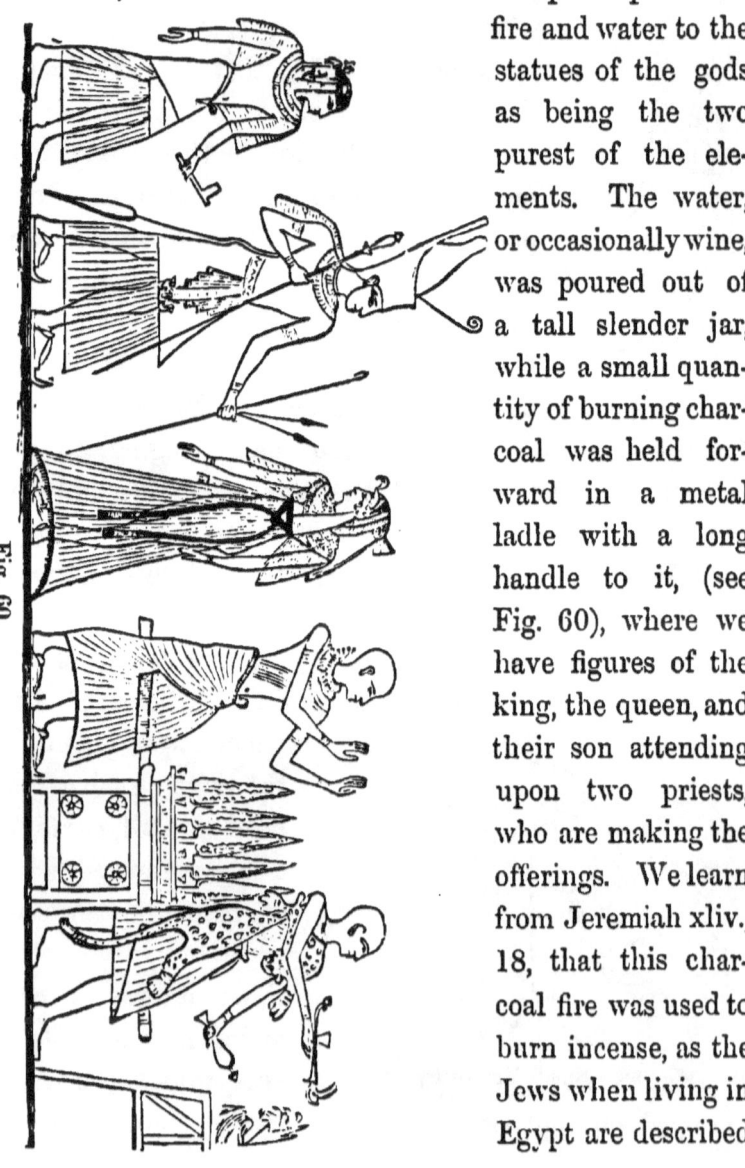

Fig. 60.

as burning incense and pouring out drink offerings to the Egyptian goddess, the Queen of Heaven, after the manner of the country.

The Egyptians were accused by the Greeks and Romans of sacrificing human beings on the altars of Osiris. But it is probable that the only foundation for the charge was a custom of accompanying the beheading of criminals with a religious ceremony, in which Osiris may have been declared the judge of the living as well as of the dead. They may perhaps have also had a custom of putting to death the criminals on days sacred to that god. Some such custom was followed by the Jews, and even by the Roman governors of Judea; as we learn from the Gospels, that at the Passover, when the Saviour was crucified, there were three criminals, a murderer, and two robbers, waiting in prison to be put to death at the same feast.

The religious character òf the Ancient Egyptians, shows itself to us even at the present day, after so many centuries, in a most marked manner by the costly way in which they made the bodies into mummies by embalmment, and by the costly tombs in which they then laid them to await the day of resurrection. Their tombs were built with more care than their houses; the tombs of their kings were often larger and more ornamented than the temples and palaces. The tombs of the kings and high priests of Memphis are huge pyramids, standing upon the western hills which divide the cultivated land from the desert. In the middle of each is a small chamber in which was placed the embalmed body enclosed in a massive granite sarcophagus. (See Fig. 61.) The pyramid takes its name from the words Pi-Rama, *The*

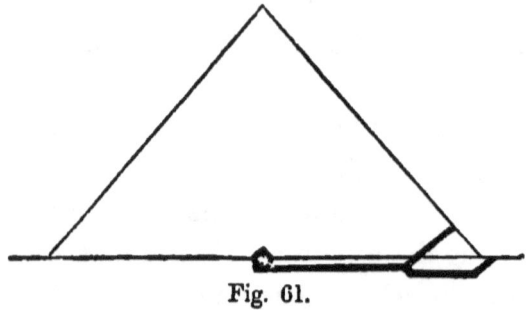

Fig. 61.

Mountain; and the Arabs, changing the Coptic article for their own, still call it by the same name, Ar-Rama. Those which are built of stone remain, and two of them are the largest, and probably the oldest buildings in the world. Those which were built of unburnt bricks have crumbled away in the last three thousand years into a heap of rubbish. In Thebes on the other hand, where the western hills are of a limestone particularly well suited for caverns, the tombs are chambers hollowed out of the hill side, beautifully sculptured and painted within, but with entrance so covered up with the soil, as to escape the notice of even the most curious eyes. The Theban kings were buried in a valley set apart for kings' tombs only, and their queens were buried in another valley, with the entrances equally concealed in the earth. The kings of Memphis meant to save their embalmed bodies from being disturbed, by the strength of the stone work in which they were encased, and the kings of Thebes by means of the care with which the entrance to the tomb was concealed. In both neighbourhoods the tombs were made in the desert, beyond the limits of the Nile's overflow, and thus beyond the cultivated fields, as in places where the mummies were least likely to decay or be disturbed. Job, who everywhere shows an acquaintance

TOMBS OF THEBES.   43

with Egyptian civilization, in Chapter iii., 14, says that the kings and counsellors of the earth built for themselves tombs in the desert; and it was after Plato had travelled in Egypt that he proposed in his Book on Laws that no human body should be buried in any spot which could be cultivated.

In Fig. 62 we have the ground plan and the vertical section of the tomb of king Oimenephah I., in the valley of kings' tombs at Thebes. When the entrance had been discovered, and eighteen feet of earth had been removed by the enterprising Belzoni, he descended through staircases and passages for about 120 feet further, till he arrived at a pit or dry well, which was thirteen feet across, and thirty feet deep, marked A in our plan. This was meant not only to bar an intruder's further progress, but to deceive him with the appearance of its being the end of the cavern. Our discoverer, however, made a bridge across this pit, and broke an opening through the wall on the opposite side, and by this he entered the chamber marked B, and then into the chamber marked C. Then returning into the chamber marked B, he descended through a flight of stairs and a passage till he reached the principal chamber, out of which five smaller chambers open. The further half of this principal chamber is vaulted, and under that vault stood the Alabaster Sarcophagus, formed to

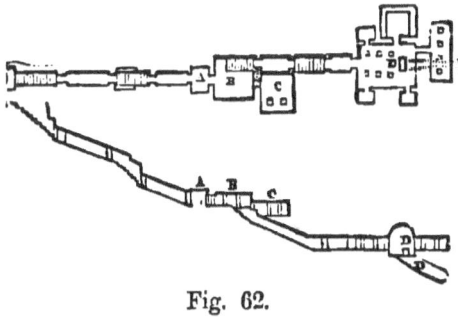

Fig. 62.

hold the body of the king, which was no doubt embalmed and placed within a first and second wooden mummy case. But the Sarcophagus had been broken open and its contents rifled, probably centuries before our discoverer had reached it. It therefore still remains doubtful whether the king was really buried with it; for under the sarcophagus was found a staircase descending three hundred feet further, and there closed by rubbish, so that it is at least possible that the king's embalmed body may be yet lying safely within a second sarcophagus, still deeper and further beneath the Theban hills.

Such was the care taken by a great king to save his earthly body unhurt and undisturbed against the day of resurrection. Equally costly and laboured were the painted sculptures against the walls of these beautiful passages and chambers. The king's soul is represented in the form of a crowned vulture with outstretched wings, and two sceptres, each an ostrich feather, in its claws. It has the king's name and titles written over it. In other sculptures the soul is a bird with a human head, as in Fig. 29 and Fig. 73. There are several groups of figures each representing the king embracing a god, placing his right arm in a loving manner round the god's neck. (See Fig. 63.) These are im

Fig. 63.

portant because unusual. Most pagan nations have boasted that they were beloved by their gods; but here the Theban king, with a more religious feeling, professes his love for the god Osiris, in return. The same feeling is shown in the name of his son Rameses II., who though usually styled Amun-mai, or *Beloved by Amun*, is sometimes called Mi-amun or *Lover of Amun*.

The serpent of evil, the great enemy of the human race, plays an important part in all pictures and sculptures relating to the next world. If its numerous spiral folds were made straight it would sometimes be an hundred and fifty feet long. When we see it in the water with a number of women around it on the river's banks, we are reminded of the Greek fable of the serpent in the garden with the daughters of Hesperus; when it is pierced through the head by the spear of the goddess Isis, we see the enmity between the woman and the serpent spoken of in Genesis, chap. iii. It is always conquered by the good, sometimes pierced through its folds by a number of swords, and sometimes carried away alive in the arms of its conquerors in triumph as in Fig. 64.

Fig. 64.

The wish for immortality or a life hereafter, and the belief that it could be obtained with the help of this earthly body and not without it, led the Egyptians to give as much care to embalming it before burial as to building its tomb. But the completeness of the embalmment, like the size and strength of the tomb, varied with the importance of the dead person and the wealth of his family. Kings and High Priests were often buried in a stone sarcophagus, which contained a first and then a second inner mummy case, both made of wood. The two inner cases were usually shaped to the body, as also was sometimes the stone sarcophagus. Some bodies were buried in only two cases, and some in only one. Sometimes all three cases were of wood, as in Fig. 65,

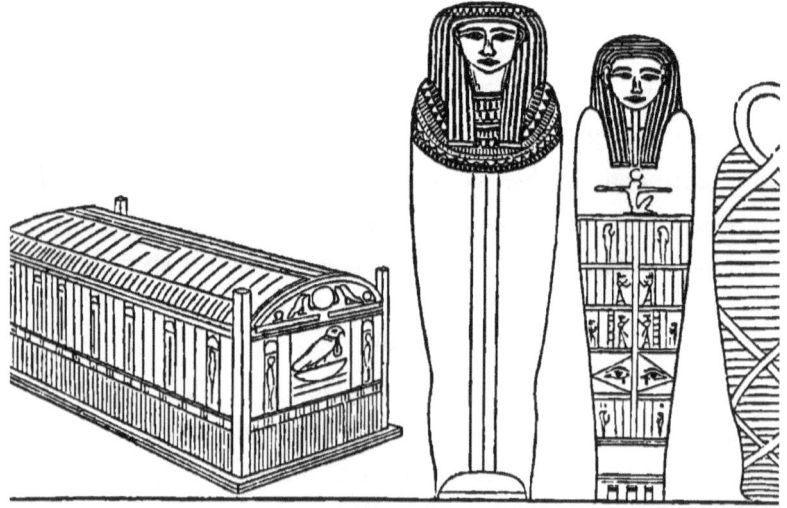

Fig. 65.

where the two inner cases are shaped to the body, with heads and faces carved and painted, while the third and outer case, is a chest with straight sides and arched top. Such a mummy case as this was meant to lie flat on the ground, but when the outer case, whether a first, second, or third, was shaped to the body, it was sometimes placed upon its feet upright against the wall. We learn from the arrangement of the sculpture on the outer case, whether it was meant to stand up or to lie down.

The inscriptions on these cases usually declare the pedigree of the deceased person through two, three, or four generations, and add a variety of religious sentences in honour of the several gods, whose figures are there painted or sculptured, and tell us that he was a righteous good man, now changed into the god Osiris, and immortal. He holds in his hands the two sceptres of that god. The mummies of women are perhaps as common as those of men; and the rank of both is usually priestly. The mummies of children are rare; if many were made they have probably long since gone to decay, together with those of the humbler classes of society, as having received a less costly and less careful embalmment. On the mummy, and within the bandages were laid small ornaments, as charms, in the form of scarabæi, eyes, hearts, fingers, nilometer land-marks, necklaces; and sometimes on each part of the body the image of the god who acted as guardian over that part. Within the mummy case was often laid a roll of papyrus, containing an account of the events which will befal the deceased in the next world, in his passage through trials and difficulties to a state of final bliss.

The manner of embalming varied with the sum of money spent upon it. The body was opened with as little cutting and injury as possible, and the less solid parts were removed. The brain was taken out through the nostrils. When the greatest care was employed, the body was thoroughly soaked for several weeks in a mineral pitch, called Mum in the hieroglyphics; and hence our word mummy. It was then wrapped round with several hundred yards of narrow linen bandages, which were more or less soaked in the same pitch, and it was not placed within its painted wooden mummy case, till the pitch was thoroughly dry. Seventy days were allowed for the time of mourning between the death and burial, of which a large part was spent upon the embalming. But as the whole time could not have been long enough for painting the wooden mummy cases and engraving the sculptures on the sarcophagus, these costly works must have been begun long before the death. The Egyptians spent forty days in embalming the patriarch Jacob, and mourned for him the usual time of seventy days. (See Genesis 1., 3.) The softer and more moist parts of the body were some of them placed in four earthen jars, called Canobic Jars, either from the city of Canopus, or from the name of the god Kneph or Cenubis. These Jars have lids in the shape of the heads of a man, an ape, a jackal, and a hawk. (See Fig. 66.) They represent the four lesser gods of the

Fig. 66.

dead, and their names seem to describe the different operations in mummy-making over which they watched. Amset, the *carpenter*, has a man's head; Hepi, the *digger*, has an ape's head; Smotef, the *shaper*, has a jackal's head; and Snouf, the *bleeder*, has a hawk's head. But the heads of the two last are sometimes changed one for another,

THE FUNERAL. 49

and sometimes, in the place of Smotef, we have Sottef, the *cutter* or *purifier*.

The goddesses Isis and Nephthys were more particularly supposed to grieve at every man's death (See Fig. 67), and the god Anubis to assist in laying out the mummy. It was always placed on a lion-shaped couch. (See Fig. 68). When placed in the mummy-case, as the death may have taken place on the east side of the Nile, while the burial places were usually on the west side, the ferrying it across the river was an important part of the funeral ceremony. It thus crossed the stream which divided life from death, and entered the region of Amenti, the abode of the dead. If the death took place on the west side of the river, the same procession by water, was conducted across the small lake or large tank, which belonged to the temple. It was not unusual to have a small model of this sacred tank, with its flights of steps leading down to the water, cut in stone, to be used as a basin for the libations in the temple. (See Fig. 69). When the mummy of the dead man had been ferried across the water, the next ceremony was his trial before the judge Osiris.

That solemn trial of every man for his conduct in this

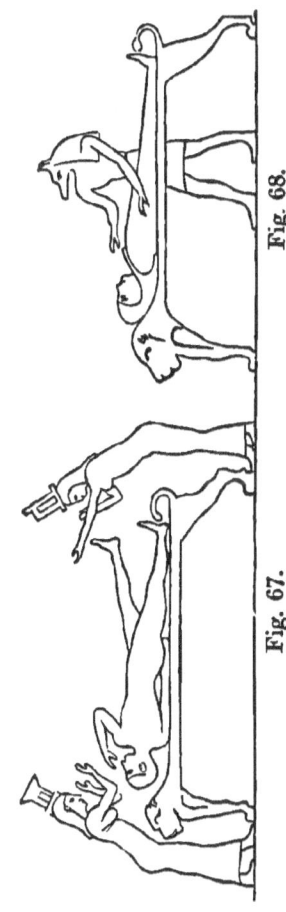

Fig. 68.

Fig. 67.

D

50   THE TRIAL SCENE.

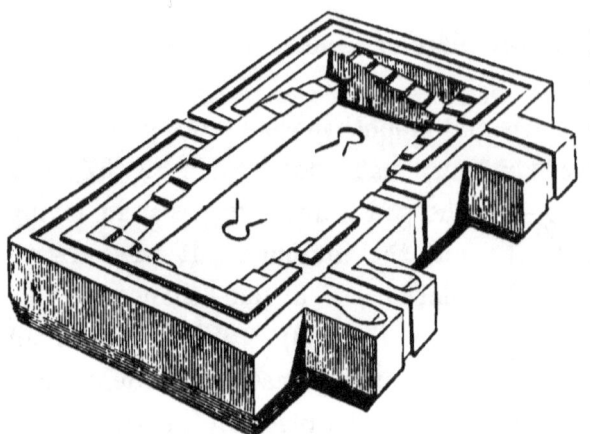

Fig. 69.

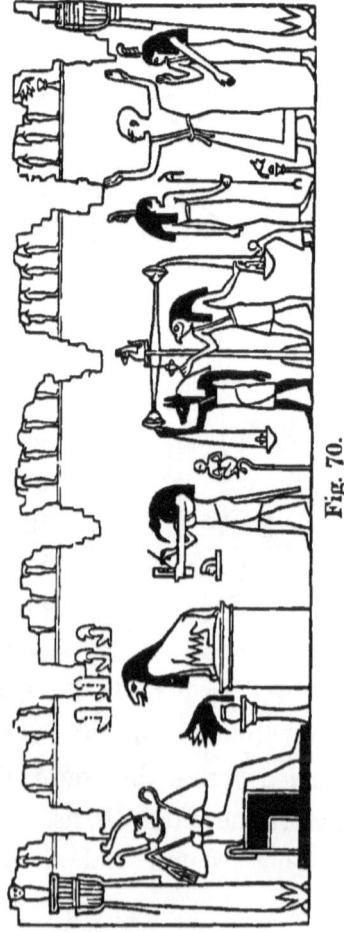

Fig. 70.

life, which was to fix his reward or punishment in the next, is one of the most interesting of the pictures on the funereal papyri, and was enacted by the priests as part of the funeral ceremony. (See Fig. 70.) They put on masks distinctive of the several gods, and thus received the body in due form. Osiris sat on a raised throne, holding his two sceptres, and wearing the crown of Upper Egypt. Before him were placed the offerings, and near him were seated the four lesser gods of the dead. The deceased holds up his hands in prayer, and is introduced by two goddesses, each wearing on her head the emblem of truth. The wicked Typhon, as an hippopotamus, the Cerberus of the Greeks, accuses him to the judge, and demands that he shall be punished; while the four lesser gods of the dead intercede as advocates or mediators on his behalf. But a large pair of scales is set up, which is quietly adjusted by the dog-headed Anubis and the hawk-headed Horus. In one scale is placed the heart or conduct of the deceased, and in the other a figure of the goddess of truth. A small weight is moved along the beam by Horus, to make the two scales balance, and to determine how much the conduct falls short of the standard weight. Forty-two assessors are at hand to assist Osiris in forming his judgment, and each declares the deceased man's innocence of that particular crime of which that assessor takes notice. The judgment when pronounced is written down by the ibis-headed Thoth, as recording angel, or god of writing. Thus are measured the goodness and the failings of the life lately ended. Those who were too uncultivated to listen to a sermon might thus learn wisdom from what they saw with their eyes, and this ceremony was a forcible method of teaching the ignorant multitude that a day of judgment awaits us all after death, and that we should so regulate our lives that when weighed in the great balance they may not be found wanting.

But notwithstanding this show of a trial, and this ceremony of the great scales, the Egyptians, like other Pagan nations, had very little trust in the justice of the Judge; and to bribe him and to appease his wrath, they prudently brought their sin-offerings, which in our figure lie upon the altar in the form of a Lotus flower. The same offerings are laid before the assessors in the hope that they also may thereby be persuaded to return favourable answers to the questions that the judge may put to them. Again the four lesser gods, who come forward as the friends and advocates of the trembling sinner, may be seen at the head of a tablet in the British Museum, strengthening their mediation on his behalf by laying their own gifts upon the altar before Osiris. (See Fig. 71). On other

Fig. 71.

tablets we see other gods joining him in his prayers as his advocates, and making their offerings jointly with him. Nor was this always thought enough to obtain from the judge a verdict in favour of the deceased. The greater the sacrifice, the greater would be the chance of a favourable verdict.

Fig. 72.

Accordingly the four lesser gods are themselves supposed to offer themselves as an atoning sacrifice on behalf of the sinner; and on a funeral tablet in the British Museum, dated in 62nd year of Rameses II. we see the deceased has placed them on the altar before Osiris, as his sin offering. (See Fig. 72).

The resurrection of the dead to a second life had been a deep rooted religious opinion among the Egyptians from the earliest times. They told Herodotus that when the soul left its own body, it took up its abode in the bodies of other animals, and was there imprisoned during a number of other short lives; and thus after passing for three thousand years through the bodies of birds, beasts, and fishes, it was again allowed to return into its old dwelling. Among the sculptures on the sarcophagus of Oimenepthah II., we see the human race mounting the steps of a lofty throne, on which is seated the Judge Osiris, with the great scales before him, and the soul of one unhappy man, who has been found guilty, has been lodged in the body of a pig, as the representative of impurity, and in that form is carried away in a boat by the god Anubis from the presence of the judge. On the other hand, on a papyrus in the British Museum we see a painting of the mummy of a good man placed inside the body of a ram, the animal sacred to the god Kneph, and thus the proper dwelling place for goodness.

The figures on the ornamental mummy cases abundantly prove to us that the reason for saving the body from decay, by embalming it as a mummy was, that it might be ready for the soul to re-enter when the years of wandering were at an end. The painting represents the mummy lying on its lion-shaped couch, with the soul returning to it, in the form of a bird with human head, and putting back life and breath into its mouth, while the god

Fig. 73.

Anubis is preparing to unwrap the bandages. (See Fig. 73). The character for life is a key, in the form of a cross with a ring at the top; that for breath is the mast and sail of a ship, which naturally remind us of wind. It was only at a late time, perhaps not till after their intercourse with the Greeks, that some few of the Egyptians entertained the opinion of a spiritual resurrection, without the help of the dead body. They show this opinion in the painting by giving to a man at the moment of his death two bodies, the one earthly and mortal, and the other angelic and immortal. (See Fig. 74). The vault of heaven is represented by the outstretched figure of the goddess Neith, painted blue. On each side sits a figure of the ram-headed Kneph, holding the feather, the character for Truth, to show that the dead man is righteous, or has been acquitted by the judge Osiris. In the middle is the earthly body, painted red, falling to the ground in death, while the heavenly body, painted blue, stands upright and holds up his hands in the attitude of prayer. This picture describes the opinion of the apostle Paul, who says in 1 Corinth. xv. 44, "There is an animal body and there is a spiritual body." But this more spiritual view of the resurrection to a future life was never generally received by the Egyptians. They clung to the old opinion of the resurrection of the body, and continued to make it into a mummy, to save it for the return of the soul. The two opinions are both spoken

Fig. 74.

of in Acts xxiii. 8, where we read that the Sadducees say there is no resurrection, neither angel nor spirit, but the Pharisees acknowledge both.

Within the family tomb were placed against the wall the sculptured and painted funereal tablets or tombstones of the persons buried there. In the best days of Thebes the funereal tablet was usually headed with the winged sun, and had a date telling us in what day of the month, and in what year of the king's reign it was set up. Beneath this we see the deceased on his knees presenting his offerings to those gods to whom he was more particularly attached. To every god is given his name and titles. The row is perhaps headed by Amun-Ra, as king of the gods, or perhaps by Osiris, the judge of the dead. Below this the deceased is making the same offerings to his ancestors, to each of whom is given his name, and relationship, and titles, which are usually priestly. Then follow several lines of hieroglyphical writing, declaring that the tablet is dedicated to the above gods, in honour of the deceased, to whom is given his titles and pedigree through a line of priests and priestesses, and adding a boastful account of his gifts to the temple of oxen, geese, wine, oil, milk, money, and other valuables. On the earliest tablets the deceased is not worshipping the gods, but is himself receiving homage from his own children, who show their piety by setting out a table of food for his use after his death.

Various were the opinions among the priests about a good man's employments and pleasures after death. Some painted him on the papyrus which was buried with him, as busy ploughing with oxen and sowing his seed in a field well watered with canals, and that needed no pumping. Others made him lie in easy idleness by the side of his water-tank, enjoying the wished for coolness and freedom from thirst. Some painted him on the wall of his tomb seated, with his staff of inheritance in his hand, while his servants are counting out before him his wealth in cattle and corn, and while his guests are feasting, with women servants handing wine to them, and others entertaining them with music. Some buried him with the prayer that he might be able to get the better of his enemies when he met them in the next world, and showed him sitting in pride with those unhappy men, who might have before offended him, now in bonds beneath his chair;

Fig. 75.

or they painted on the mummy case the same enemies with their arms tied behind them under the soles of his feet to be trampled on. (See Fig. 75.)

Many of these opinions about the resurrection and a future state of rewards and punishments, were borrowed by the Greeks directly from Egypt, as we see by the Egyptian names which they took with the opinions. Thus Rro-t-amenti, or *King of Hell*, the title of Osiris, gave a name to Rhadamanthus, the Greek judge of the dead. Menes, the fabulous founder of the Egyptian monarchy, became Minos, a second judge of the dead. From the word Charo, *silent*, the boatman of Greek mythology, who ferried the dead into the next world, was called Charon, and the river which he crossed was called Acheron. Hecate, *the sorceress*, one of the titles of Isis, was given by the Greeks and Romans as a name to their queen of Hell. The hippopotamus who stands before Osiris, when he is judging the dead in Fig. 70, p. 50, is one of the Cabeiri gods, and became among the Greeks, with but little change in figure and name, the dog Cerberus. The goddess Thmei, or *truth*, with the ostrich head in the same figure, became the Greek Themis, or goddess of justice. Those who are less in earnest are usually led in their opinions by the more grave and serious. Herodotus tells us that though he did not believe much that was told him on these matters, yet that he thought them too serious to relate in his book. And thus the Greeks, as soon as Egypt was open to them by the rise of a race of kings at Sais, who favoured Greek intercourse, readily copied the more solemn of the Egyptian superstitions.

Nileometer Landmark.

Fig. 76.

THE RELIGION OF LOWER EGYPT.

After the fall of Thebes, after the conquest of Egypt by the Ethiopians, and after the disorders which followed thereupon, we find in about the year B.C. 700, a race of kings, who made Sais in the Delta their capital, sovereigns of all Egypt. After their rise, we note a considerable change in the Egyptian religion as it appears upon the more modern monuments. This may have arisen from any or all of three causes. First, during the late troublous centuries, while fewer monuments were made, the religion of the nation may have been slowly undergoing a change, which now at length shows itself on the monuments. Or, secondly, as frailer records, such as wooden mummy cases and the papyri inclosed therein, have been saved to us in greater numbers, from these more modern times, while the older Theban records are mostly sculptures on the stone walls, it is very possible that a different class of sentiments may be thereby shown to us. Or, thirdly, the people of Lower Egypt, having always been somewhat of a different race from those of Upper Egypt, may have always had in many points a different religious opinion.

The western half of the Delta, had received a considerable colony of Greek traders, and hence arose a mixed population, half Egyptian and half Greek; and in the eastern half of the Delta there was a yet larger number of Jewish and Phenician settlers, from the latter of whom sprung a population half Egyptian and half Phenician. Naucratis in the west was wholly a Greek city, and Sais the western capital, was very much under Greek influence. On the other side, Isaiah tells us that there were as many as five cities on the Pelusiac, or eastern branch of the Nile, where Hebrew was the language spoken in the streets. Pelusium was wholly peopled by Phenician sailors, and so numerous were they in Memphis, that one part of the city was called the Tyrian quarter. Though the Greeks introduced many new arts into Egypt, they probably brought about no change in the religion; in religious matters they were always happy to learn from the Egyptians. Far otherwise was the case with the Phenicians; and many of the gods worshipped at Memphis were considered by Herodotus to be Phenician deities. Hence it is probable that the religion of Lower Egypt was largely coloured with Phenician opinions. At any rate from which ever of the above causes it arose, we now find more frequent and stronger proofs that the gods were worshipped in fear rather than in love; that the sacrifices were made less than they used to be in thankfulness for blessings received, and more often than formerly, as an atonement to turn aside punishment that is dreaded. Pthah, the great god of Memphis, is now an ugly dwarf, with an enlarged head, (see Fig. 77), and he sometimes holds a club over his head, as if in the act of threatening

Fig. 77.

Fig. 78.

his worshippers with vengeance. (See Fig. 78). He is the father of a brood of children, as ugly and as malicious as himself. These are the Cabeiri, whose office it was to torture the wicked who may be found guilty by Osiris at the great trial on the day of Judgment. Their name is derived from the Egyptian word KBA, *punishment*, and IRI, *to do*, as Osiris from OSH, *a decree*, and IRI, *to do*. As we have before mentioned, Typhon, the hippopotamus, the accuser in the trial-scene, page 50, was one of them. For the purpose of torturing their victims, they are armed with swords, snakes, and lizards, as in Fig. 79, where they

Fig. 79.

accompany their father Pthah, with his enlarged head. One of them is represented in the form of a gibbet, armed with a sword, with a human head hanging from it, and near them is the bottomless pit and lake of fire, into which their victims are to be thrown. It is guarded by an ape sitting at each corner. The painted papyri, which have been found in the mummy cases, show us these disagreeable imps and their victims in endless variety; but at the same time they always tell us that the fortunate man, who had been rich enough to have his body embalmed in a costly manner, and the ceremonies on his

THE CABEIRI.

funeral drawn and painted on the papyrus, has escaped their clutches. On the beautiful papyrus at Leyden, published by Dr. Lemans, we see that the deceased, or else the gods who befriend him, have succeeded in overcoming the eleven Cabeiri, and imprisoning them in as many cells. In the yet larger papyrus at Turin, published by Dr. Lepsius, these cells, or prisons, are shewn to be caverns, some underground, with trees on the top of them, and some under the valley of the river, with the Nile-gods seated on the top. In this papyrus, the Cabeiri are twenty-one or twenty-two in number, and Kneph, with the ram's head, would seem to be the god, who helped the deceased to imprison them. On the monuments of the city of Sais, the kings are not like those of Thebes, presenting their offerings to Ammon Ra, but to these threatening Cabeiri. Fig. 80 represents Pharaoh Hophra on his knees, presenting two cones of baked clay, typical of his gifts, to one of these monsters, with a double bull's head, as an atoning sacrifice on behalf of the nation, to turn aside the threatened punishment.

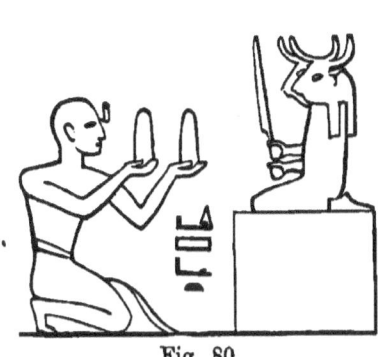

Fig. 80.

This fear of future punishment sometimes made the priests set the hated Typhon, the hippopotamus, who was one of the Cabeiri, at the head of a funereal tablet, as a divinity who was to be appeased with gifts. Herodotus tells us that these Cabeiri were more particularly the gods of the Phenician settlements in the Delta, but from the papyri we learn that their worship was common to all the natives of Lower Egypt.

Another Phenician deity is the foreign Venus, chiefly worshipped at Memphis, who, unlike the Egyptian goddessess, is wholly unclothed. She is Athor under a new form, having her long hair falling in two locks on her shoulders, and having a basket on her head. (See Fig. 81). She shows us a front view, and stands upon a lion that walks sideways. She stands between two gods, each on the top of a small temple with a door. One is the Egyptian Chem, who with his right arm raised holds the whip. The other is a foreign god, with an Asiatic beard: he holds a spear in his right hand, and the character for life in his left hand. In place of the sacred Asp, the usual ornament of a god's forehead, he has a dog's or stag's head with two long ears, like that on the top of an Anubis-staff. The name of

Fig. 81.

the goddess is Koun, the queen of Heaven; the name of the foreign god is Ranpo, Lord of Heaven, and king of the other gods. To Chem, the goddess presents a bunch of flowers, emblems of life, and to the foreign god two serpents, emblems of death, thus declaring the Gnostic and Manichean doctrine of Antitheses or oppositions between life and death, or good and evil, a doctrine of which we see many more traces in Lower Egypt than in the Thebaid. The goddess Koun, or Chiun, is mentioned by the prophet Amos, in chapter v. 26, where the Greek translators in the Septuagint version, have changed her name into Raephan, which in Acts vii. 43, is spelled Remphan; and thus by a strange change we have these two Phenician deities both mentioned in the same sentence. This god Ranpo is sculptured on other Egyptian monuments, with a spear and shield in one hand, and a battle-axe in the other, with which he is prepared to strike down his terrified worshippers.

The goddess Anaita, who is mentioned by Strabo as a Persian goddess, was another divinity, whom the people of Memphis supplicated to withhold her punishments. She wears the crown of Osiris, and at the bottom of the tablet Fig. 81, p. 62, she is threatening to destroy with her battle-axe the worshippers who have covered her altar with their various offerings. But the human mind, when it has created for itself so much to be feared, by a natural effort creates for itself also a protector. At Sais, this protector was the goddess Neith, to whom the worshipper turned in love and hope, when he had frightened himself with the belief, that even the hated Typhon might take the place of his judge, and that Anaita and Rampo were waiting to attack him, and the Cabeiri to torture him and thrust him into the pit of fire. Every king of Sais, professed that he was beloved by Neith, as the kings of Thebes said they were beloved by Amun-Ra. The people of Lower Egypt lived under the shadow of her wings, (see Fig. 67, page 58), as the people of Upper Egypt lived under the winged sun (see Fig. 1, page 1).

It is to the later times of Egyptian history, perhaps to the five centuries immediately before the Christian era, that the religious opinions contained in the funereal papyri chiefly belong. The roll of papyrus buried with the mummy often describes the funeral, and then goes on to the return of the soul to the body, the resurrection, the various trials and difficulties which the deceased will meet and overcome in the next world, and the garden of paradise in which he awaits the day of judgment, the trial on that day, and it then shows the punishment which would have awaited him if he had been found guilty. The papyrus is five, ten, twenty, or even sixty feet in length. It is divided into chapters of hieratic writing, each headed with a picture. First, we see the grief for his death. The men hold up their hands in prayer, the women throw dust upon their heads, and all beat their breasts. The mummy is placed in a boat and ferried across the sacred lake. The goddesses Isis and Nephthys, in the boat with it, hang over it in grief. The procession moves forward to the temple, in front of which stand two obelisks. The priests carry a variety of standards, each an image of a god on a pole, and lead with them an animal for the sacrifice. In front of the temple a bountiful offering is made of food, birds, beasts, fishes, fruits, bread, and wine

There the mummy is received with the honours due to such costly gifts, and is placed in its tomb, by the side of which stands the tombstone. Then begin the events of the next life. The deceased in the boat of Ra, on his knees before the threefold Horus, presents his offering to these gods. Again he joins his wife in worshipping the sun, while four apes worship another figure of the same god, and a priest presents to him and his wife fire and water, as divine honours. Before his journey he addresses his prayers to the various gods, and then enters upon his labours. He attacks with spear in hand the crocodiles, lizards, scorpions, and snakes which beset his path, and passing through these dark regions he at length reaches the land of Amenti, whose goddess is a hawk standing upon a perch. Here the sun's rays cheer his steps, and he meets among other wonders the head of Horus rising out of a Lotus flower, the god Pthah, the phœnix, his own soul in the form of a bird with human head, and the goddess Isis as a serpent of goodness. The soul then returns to the mummy and puts life into its mouth. He then enters upon his farm, floating upon one of the canals in a boat, and passing by the land mark at its boundary. In this farm he ploughs, he sows the seed, he reaps the corn, and presents his offerings to the god of the Nile who fills the canals with water. Then follow his prayers to numerous gods and temples. At length arrives the day of judgment, and he is brought before the god Osiris and his forty-two assessors, to have his conduct weighed in the great scales, as described in page 50. After the trial we are shown the lake of fire into which the wicked are to be thrown, and the gods of punishment, the Cabeiri, with swords in their hands. These, however, do him no injury, they are in his case overcome, and each safely imprisoned in a cell under ground, or under the river Nile.

Sometimes the tree of life, with the goddess Neith in its branches, is one of the trees in the paradise which the deceased enters. Sometimes he only reaches this happy land after his trial and acquittal, instead of being allowed to wait there until the day of judgment. Sometimes we see more of the punishment of the wicked, their heads are hanging from posts, their bodies imprisoned in caves, or they are awaiting their punishment with their arms tied behind them. Some papyri explain the transmigration of souls, as before mentioned, and show us the good man within the body of a ram, and the wicked man driven away in the form of a pig.

The religious earnestness of the Egyptians was unfortunately accompanied with the same fault that it carries with it in modern times, namely religious intolerance, from which Greeks and Romans were far more free. The people of Marea and Apis, on the banks of the Lake Mareotis, who were Libyians, and did not hold the religious opinions of the Egyptians, saw nothing wicked in eating beef, and did not like to be forbidden to kill a cow in their own cities. They pleaded that they were not Egyptians. But they could obtain no religious toleration from their rulers; they might kill and eat buffaloes, but they were not allowed to keep oxen for their own eating, because in drinking out of their lake they drank the sacred waters of the Nile. In some cases the Egyptians seem to have wished even to force their religion upon unwilling neighbours. When king Shishank had defeated Rehoboam, King of Judah, and made Jeroboam king of the northern tribes of Israel, it would seem that the golden calves set up by both sovereigns were acts of homage to the Egyptian conqueror. The spread of the emblems of Egyptian religion in Etruria, and in the islands of Cyprus, Malta, and Sardinia, must be owing to the peaceable intercourse by trade, through the vessels of the Phenicians, rather than to any act of violence; and indeed it was again and again remarked by the Greeks, that such was the serious nature of the Egyptian superstitions, that they conquered and put down every other superstition that they came near.

The Egyptian's opinion of the creation was the growth of his own river's bank. The thoughtful man, who saw the Nile every year lay a body of solid manure upon his field, was able to measure against the walls of the old temples that the ground was slowly but certainly rising. An increase of the earth was being brought about by the river. Hence he readily believed that the world itself had of old been formed "out of water, and by means of water," as described in 2 Peter iii. 5. The philosophers were nearly of the same opinion. They held that matter was itself eternal, like the other gods, and that our world, in the beginning, before it took any shape upon itself, was like thin mud, or a mass of water containing all things that where afterwards to be brought forth out of it. When the water had by its divine will separated itself from the earth, then the great Ra, the sun, sent down his quickening heat, and plants and animals came forth out of the wet land, as the insects are spawned out of the fields, before the eyes of the husbandman, every autumn after the Nile's overflow has retreated. The crafty priests of the Nile, who had lived in confinement as monks, declared that they had themselves visited and dwelt in the caverns beneath the river, where these treasures, while yet unshaped, were kept in store and waiting to come into being. And on the days sacred to the Nile, boys, the children of priestly families, were every year dedicated to the blue river-god that they might spend their youth in monastic retirement, and as it was said, in these caverns beneath his waves. The sarcophagus of Oimenepthah represents the earth as a round plain, encircled by the body of Osiris, and floating in the ocean, while the goddess Neith, *the heavens*, stands upon the head of Osiris to increase the height, and thus holds up the sun. At the same time a large figure of the ocean rises out of the water and holds up with his two hands the boat of Ra, in which the sun is carried. That these were very early Egyptian opinions, we learn from our finding traces of them in the oldest of the Hebrew Scriptures, though the writers there are not so far warped by them as to rob the Creator of the praise for his own works. The author of the book of Genesis tells us that the Almighty formed our earth and its inhabitants by dividing the land from the water, and then commanding them both to bring forth living creatures; and again one of the Psalmists says that his substance, while yet imperfect, was by the Creator curiously wrought in the lowest depths of the earth. The Hebrew writer, however, is never misled, so far as to think that any part of the creation was its own creator. But in the Egyptian philosophy, sunshine and the river Nile are themselves the divine agents; and hence fire and water received divine honours, as the two purest of the elements, and every day when the temple of Serapis in Alexandria was opened, the singer standing on the steps of the portico sprinkled water over the marble floor while he held forth fire to the people (See Fig. 82) and though he and most of his hearers were Greeks, he called upon the god in the Egyptian language. A vase of water or sometimes of wine, and metal cup containing a small charcoal fire, were often presented to the altar, as figurative of divine honours. (See Fig. 60.)

Fig. 82.

Tomb with an arch.

THE RELIGION
UNDER THE
PERSIAN CONQUERORS.

THE Persians, on their conquest of Egypt, in the year B.C. 523, began with insulting the Egyptians in their religious feelings, by killing the bull Apis, and by breaking to pieces the statues of the gods. They afterwards made an earnest attempt to bring about some changes in the religion, and the chief was to abolish the worship of all statues and figures of the gods, and to introduce the more simple worship of the sun. Of this we see traces in the sculptures, made by a native Satrap, who governed the country under Artaxerxes Longimanus. (See Fig. 83.) We there see Thaomra, the son of the late king Adon-Ra Bakan, or Thannyras, the son of Inarus, as Herodotus calls him, worshipping the sun, Adon-Ra which is distinguished from the sun of the Egyptians, by the absence of wings or asps, and by its sending forth a

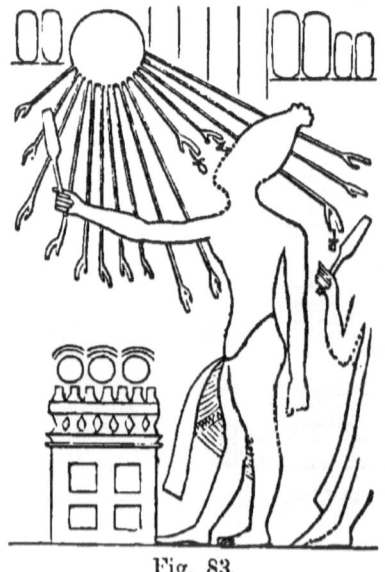

Fig. 83.

SUN WORSHIP.

number of rays, each
ending with a human
hand, and yet more par-
ticularly by the absence
of the human figure or
statue of the god. In
this the sculptor borrows
a figure from the name of
the Persian king, who
was called Longimanus,
because his arm was sup-
posed to reach over Asia,
Africa, and part of Eu-

Fig. 84.

rope. And when we see a sculpture with one of the early
Theban kings worshipping the figure of Amun-Ra, with
the same sun, as in (Fig. 84), we may suppose that the
rays ending in human hands were an after addition made
by order of the Persians.

It was in the fourth century before the Christian era
that Plato, the Athenian, visited Egypt to study at Heliopolis, where was then a celebrated school of philosophy.
The country was at the time independent, and under the
rule of a native sovereign, but it had been for a century
oppressed by the Persian conquerors. Heliopolis was on
the Phenician side of the Delta, in the neighbourhood of
the district inhabited by the Jews, who by this time had
very much acquired the use of the Greek language, from
the colonists on the other side of the Delta. Hence
Greek, Hebrew, Phenician, Persian, and Egyptian opinions
had been there freely brought into comparison, and the
consequence was a burst of free thought which made

Heliopolis for a time an important centre of learning. That Plato's opinions were very much the fruit of his visit to this celebrated school is clear from his writings. Here he may have gained better views of a future state of rewards and punishment; but here he may have lost somewhat of the pure morality before taught to him by Socrates. He seems to have been more particularly pleased with the Egyptian mysticism. But had Plato's philosophy died with himself it would claim little notice here; it is the writings of his followers that make us note its rise as important in the history of Egyptian opinions.

" Pharaoh Thaomra, his name successor to Adonra."

THE RELIGION UNDER THE PTOLEMIES.

AFTER the conquest of Egypt by the Greeks in the year B.C. 332, and on the building of the Greek city of Alexandria, Heliopolis lost much of its importance as a school. Alexandria then became the seat of that mixture of opinions which had made Heliopolis famous. The Jews there gained yet further acquaintance with Greek literature, and gave to the Greeks some knowledge of the Hebrew Bible. The Greeks of Alexandria embraced many of the Egyptian views of religion, and some of them even entered the Egyptian temples as priests, and lived under all the austerities of the Egyptian monastic rules. Greeks and Egyptians intermarried; and the children of these mixed marriages, who were declared to be Egyptians, not Greeks, carried many Greek opinions into the Egyptian religion. Under Greek toleration, as we learn from the sculptures, the Theban temples freed themselves from the intrusion of gods from Lower Egypt. In Alexandria we find Platonism becoming every year more mystical, or if we may say so, more Egyptian and less Greek. We find traces of it in the Septuagint, and in the Apocryphal Book of Jesus the son of Sirach, and in the Book of Wisdom, and in the works of Philo, all written in Egypt. When Christianity rises into notice in Alexandria, it in the same way always wears somewhat of a Platonic dress, as we see in the writings of Athenagoras, Clemens, and Origen. The quarrel between the Christian sects in Egypt arises always from the struggle between the Greek and Egyptian opinions, or rather the struggle how far Christianity, which entered Egypt as a Greek religion, and which readily met the Egyptian opinions so far as to ally itself with the new Platonism—how far it will yet further consent to become Egyptian.

In the Hebrew Scriptures we find frequent mention of Egypt, of its wars, and of its arts and civilization. The ornaments of its temple worship are sometimes copied, while its idolatry and superstition are again and again forbidden in the Mosaic laws. But we find very few traces of the Hebrew writers having borrowed any Egyptian opinions, except in the second and third chapters of Genesis, where the garden of Eden is watered like Egypt without rain; where there is a sacred tree of Life, and another of the knowledge of good and evil; where the serpent is able to speak, and tempts the woman to sin, and is declared to be the enemy of the human race; and where the door of the garden is guarded by a cherub, or one of the Cabeiri, with a flaming sword, lest the sinner should approach the tree of Life. But, in more modern times, we become acquainted with a body of Jews who had been for centuries living in Egypt, and were no longer confined to their own towns, on the eastern branch of the Nile. They had learned the use of the Greek language, and were thence called Hellenists; and among them we find many philosophical and even religious opinions, which owe their origin to the Egyptian priests among whom they were living. They received a wise patronage from the

Ptolemies, who founded the museum of learning in Alexandria. In the third century before the Christian era, some of them translated the Hebrew Scriptures into Greek, for the use of their brethren who were less acquainted with Hebrew; and the translators often show a leaning towards opinions very foreign from those of the original writers. In the disputed question of the age of the world, in order to make it better agree with Egyptian history, they add largely to the age of each patriarch at the time of his son's birth, thus making the world older by an Egyptian cycle, of four times 365 years. They lessened the number of years during which the children of Jacob dwelt in Egypt, by 175 years, in which they may have been justified by the Egyptian records, though they neglected their duty as faithful translators. In the Book of Zechariah, the translator's knowledge of the climate leads him to omit the threat against the Israelites in Egypt, that they shall have no rain if they come not up to Jerusalem to the feast. The translator of the Chronicles, changes the name of the great Jewish feast in a manner that gives to the word an Egyptian etymology, instead of a Jewish. He calls it not Pascha, the *passing over*, but Pasek, the *leading forth*.

As the Jews in their Greek translation of the Bible, thought fit to accept from the Egyptians and to introduce some improvements as they might call them, into the Chronology, so they were not willing to be behindhand in mysticism and spiritual refinements. By a refinement of criticism, they sometimes found more meaning in their scriptures than had ever entered the minds of the writers. Thus when the Psalmist, speaking of the power of

Jehovah, says, with a truly eastern figure (Psalm civ. 4), *He maketh the winds his messengers and the lightnings his servants*, these translators change the sentence into a philosophical description of the spiritual nature of angelic beings, and say, *He maketh his angels into spirits and his servants into a flame of fire.* Again, when Isaiah (chap. xi. 2), describes the spirit of the Lord, as *a Spirit of wisdom and understanding, a Spirit of counsel and might, a Spirit of knowledge and godly fear*, the Jews of Egypt made these six qualities of the mind, into six angelic beings, which had proceeded from the Almighty, and they added a Spirit of piety, to complete the mystic number of seven, which, with the Almighty himself, afterwards made the Ogdoad. We have seen in our notice of the gods of the Egyptians, as learned from the monuments, how they often supposed that a god divided himself into two, three, or more characters, which may have given rise to this opinion of spiritual beings proceeding from the Almighty. But we now begin to see hints of some at least among the Egyptians beginning to reject polytheism, and to declare that all their numerous gods were only so many characters of the one Almighty, or else inferior beings which proceeded out of him. Osiris-Apis, or Serapis, the judge of the dead, by becoming the chief of the numerous gods, was making some approach to being the sole god. The Alexandrian Jews seem to have had in their mind this Egyptian system of defending polytheism by declaring that it was only a Plurality in Unity, when they translated Deuteronomy vi. 4. We there read in the Hebrew, *Jehovah is our God, Jehovah alone;* but the Greek translation says, *The Lord our God is one Lord*, meaning simple and undivided, as opposed to a unity formed of plurality. At the same time the Greek translators removed from their Bible some words which declare that God appeared upon earth in a human form to Moses and his companions; and they alter Exodus xxiv. 10, 11, to make it say that they saw, not the Almighty, but only the place on which he stood to speak to them. In these two cases, the translators, instead of making any approach to the Egyptian opinions, retreated yet farther from them.

The opinions of the Egyptians show themselves equally clearly in two of the Apocryphal books of the Bible, which were written by Jews living in Lower Egypt, perhaps in Alexandria; namely, The Wisdom of the Son of Sirach, and The Wisdom of Solomon. The Egyptians had believed that some of their gods, and particularly the four lesser gods of the dead, acted as mediators with the Judge Osiris, to turn aside his wrath and the punishment for their sins, and they thought that even their kings had power to do them the same service. No similar opinion appears in the Hebrew Bible; the prophets never speak of any mediator or intercessor as standing between man and his Maker; but the Son of Sirach, misquoting the last words of the Hebrew prophet Malachi, says, that Elijah was taken up to heaven for the purpose of acting as a mediator to pacify the wrath of God's judgment before it break forth into fury, and to turn his heart towards his children (chap. xlviii. 10.) This writer also follows the proverbs of Solomon in his strong figurative expression in praise of Wisdom, whom he makes into a person created before the world, who says, "I am the mother of love, and fear, and knowledge, and holy hope."

In the second of these two books, The Wisdom of Solomon, God's Word and God's Wisdom, are both spoken of in terms yet more befitting a person. God is said to have made all things by his Word, and to have ordained man by his Wisdom (chap. ix. 1). And again, Wisdom was said to have been with him when he made the world (chap. ix. 9), and his Word afterwards to have leaped down from heaven as a fierce man of war, to punish the Egyptians (xviii. 15). In this way these Alexandrian Jews, making use of bold figures of speech, not unusual in the Hebrew poets, at the same time indulging themselves in a love for Egyptian mysticism, introduce us to a trinity, of God, his Wisdom, and his Word. This is the Trinity described by Theophilus Bishop of Antioch, who is the first Christian writer who makes use of that term, since so common in controversial divinity. This is also the Trinity of Pistis Sophia, a Coptic treatise of a later age, which describes the penitential hymns which Wisdom sang at the Creation, and which the Word afterwards conveyed to mankind. It is a Trinity of the Almighty and two of his attributes, and it helped to prepare the minds of the Alexandrians for the Arian Trinity of the third century, and the Athanasian Trinity of the fourth century.

Philo, the eloquent Jew of Alexandria, shows an Egyptian fondness for the mystical properties of numbers, and for finding an allegory or secondary meaning in the plainest narrative. He thus makes the Old Testament speak a meaning more agreeable to the modern views of religion. He says that Abraham's wife Sarah is Wisdom, while Hagar is Instruction, who, after being banished, is recalled by the Word in the form of an angel; and he elsewhere explains God's Word to be his first begotten Son, by whom he governs the world. He was the first Jewish writer that applied to the Deity the mystical notion of the Egyptians that everything perfect has three parts. Speaking of the Creator, he says that there are three orders, of which the best is the Being that is, and that he has two ancient powers near him, one on the one side and one on the other, the one on the right hand being called God, and the one on the left Lord; and that the middle divinity, accompanied on each side by his powers, presents to the enlightened mind sometimes one image and sometimes three. Philo's writings thus explain to us how Platonism became united to Judaism, and again show us several points of agreement between the New Platonists and the Platonic Christians, and jointly, with the "Wisdom of Solomon," teach us the steps by which the Egyptian doctrines of plurality in unity, and of everything perfect having three parts, found their way first into the Alexandrian philosophy, Jewish as well as Pagan, and then into Christianity, and at last established the Christian Trinity.

From Philo also we learn that a large body of Egyptian Jews had embraced the monastic rules and the life of self-denial, which we have already noted among the Egyptian priests. They bore the name of Therapeutæ. They spent their time in solitary meditation and prayer, and only saw one another on the seventh day. They did not marry; the women lived the same solitary and religious life as the men. Fasting and mortification of the flesh were the foundation of their virtues. They thus introduced into the neighbourhood of Alexandria a way of life, which though common among the Egyptians, had been unknown in that dissipated city.

The Eleusinian mysteries had been introduced into Alexandria from Greece about 300 years before the Christian era. But it seems probable that they were then only returning to their native soil. What little is known of them seems to be of Egyptian origin, coloured by the Greeks, Egyptian grossness cloaked over by Greek elegance. The temple dedicated to Ceres and Proserpine stood in the south-east quarter of the city, which was thence called the Eleusinis; and there the priestesses, a troop of young women, were to be seen carrying the sacred basket through the streets and singing hymns in honour of the goddess; while they charged all profane persons, who met the procession, to keep their eyes upon the ground, lest they should see the basket and the priestesses, who were too pure for them to look upon. What was shut up in the basket was of course a secret meant never to be known beyond the walls of the temple; and it is only after two centuries that we learn from a coin of Asia Minor (see Fig 85,) that this sacred basket held a serpent, the enemy of the human race, who introduced sin and death into the world. This is the serpent of which we have seen the conquest in page 45, the serpent of the third chapter of Genesis, which misled Eve, and the Serpent of wickedness of the Gnostics. Within the temple the hierophant wore the dress and mask of the god Kneph, the crier the mask of Thoth, the priest at the altar the emblem of the moon, while another with the dress of Ra carried a torch.

Fig. 85.

The celebration of these mysteries, whatever their meaning was, was said to be a screen for immorality and vice, and probably with much truth.

Alexandria under the Ptolemies, a Greek city built on Egyptian soil, and colonised by strangers who were courted to settle there, shows a strange mixture of European, Asiatic, and Egyptian civilizations. There the religious opinions and the philosophy of all these nations were alike patronised by the sovereign, and alike struggled for mastery, and in some minds moulded themselves into union. Political despotism was there united with freedom of philosophic thought, active trade with industrious scholarship, credulity with scepticism, Egyptian superstitions with Greek satire, the self-denying asceticism of the Jewish Therapeutæ with the immoralities of the Eleusinian mysteries, the science and cold criticism of one half of the Museum, with the imaginative Platonism of the other. There flourished in particular, mathematics, astronomy, chemistry, anatomy, verbal criticism, together with fortune-telling, mysticism, and scoffing. The despotism of the sovereign checked all lofty aims after moral excellence; but the toleration, or rather impartial patronage, which descended like an heirloom with the crown, allowed such a free play to speculative opinions in religion and philosophy, as the world has never seen in any other country, or at any other time whatever. This was in part interrupted by the wars in Judea, during which the Egyptian Jews rebelled against the government, and blood was often shed in the streets of Alexandria. But if this political warfare in some respects took the form of religious persecution by the government, it very little disturbed the minds of the Alexandrian men of letters. The Greeks in that city were too little in earnest, too indifferent to all opinions to be intolerant of any, till Christianity gave a new importance to religion, and it became a bond of union between Egyptian slave and Greek freeman, which clogged the hitherto unchecked despotism of the rulers.

The Bull Apis on Coins of Cyprus.

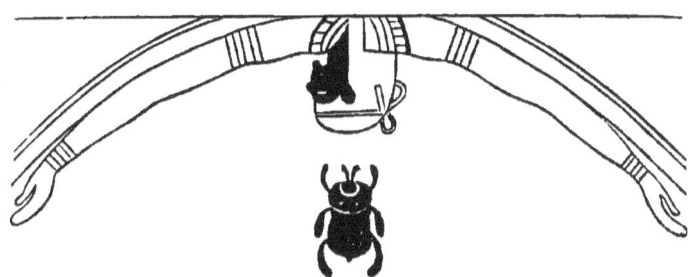

Fig. 86.—Horus as the Vault of Heaven.

THE RELIGION UNDER THE ROMANS.

DURING the two or three centuries before the Christian era, Osiris the judge of the dead, in his character of Osiris-Apis, or Serapis, had risen to a higher rank in the Egyptian mythology, and had been personified by the Ptolemies in Alexandria as the chief of the gods. He had at the same time become more a god to be feared, of which we shall see clearer proof when we come to speak of the Gnostics, when he will appear as the god of evil, under the form of the wicked serpent. This seems to have turned the worshippers towards other gods, who might shield them from his severity and wrath; and it led them to seek another judge, whom they might look upon with love. Such friends they found in the goddess Isis and her son Horus, who then took that place in their affections which, under the kings of Sais, had been held by the goddess Neith. Horus in one of his three characters, that of the Scarabæus, takes the place of Amun-Ra, the all-seeing god; and we find the vault of heaven represented not by the outstretched wings of either that god of Thebes, or of Neith the queen of Sais, but by the two arms of Horus, with the head hanging downwards, as the Almighty is painted by some of the early Italian masters. (See Fig. 86). At the same time, either alone, or in his three characters of Horus the king, Horus the scarabæus, and Horus-Ra, he sits in the sacred barge, which used to be filled with either Amun-Ra or Kneph-Ra. To Horus, with the head of a hawk, is then given the two sceptres of Osiris, and he is sometimes worshipped on the funereal papyri as the judge of the dead in place of his father. The sinner hopes to find more mercy at the judgment seat of the son. He then even rises over his father, and becomes the more important of the two in the minds of the worshippers. On a mummy case in the British Museum, where Horus is seated on the throne, holding the two sceptres of the judge, Osiris and Isis are standing before him as gods of lower rank.

Fig. 87.

At times he forms one of a trinity in unity with Ra and Osiris, as in Fig. 87, a god with the two sceptres of Osiris, the hawk's head of Horus, and the sun of Ra. This is the god described to Eusebius, who tells us that when the oracle was consulted about the divine nature, by those who wished to understand this complicated mythology, it had answered "I am Apollo and Lord and Bacchus," or to use the Egyptian names—" I am Ra and Horus and Osiris." Another god, in the form of a porcelain idol to be worn as a charm, shows us Horus as one of a trinity in unity, in name at least agreeing with that afterwards adopted by the Christians, namely, the

Great God, the Son God, and the Spirit God. In Fig. 88, the ugly grotesque human body is that of the great Pthah, the hawk's wings are those of the child Horus, and the ram's head is that of Kneph, the Spirit. But the favourite character of Horus is that of the Son.

Fig. 88.

Instead of being a crowned king, the avenger of his father, he becomes a young man, or rather a child, with a finger on his mouth, as if he had not yet learned to talk, as in Fig. 89. He is sometimes seated, as a baby, within the leaves of a lotus flower, representing the rising sun; and even while a baby, holds the sceptres of Osiris as judge of the dead. Among the porcelain images, made to be worn as charms, and to be tied round the neck with a string, he is often a child in his mother's arms. (See Fig. 90.)

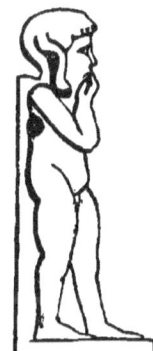

Fig. 89.

This worship of Osiris, or Serapis, as the wrathful god to be feared, and of Isis and Horus, as the merciful gods to be loved, was at its height when Antony and Cleopatra were conquered by Augustus, and Egypt became a Roman province. With the obelisks, the statues, and the gold, which were carried to Rome, were at the same time taken the Egyptian superstitions, and by many they were as much valued. Horace tells us that the beggar at the corner of the street in Rome, would then ask the passers by for alms in the name

Fig. 90.

of the holy Osiris; and Juvenal says, that the painters of that city almost lived upon the goddess Isis, such was the popularity of that most winning form of worship, which is still continued there in the pictures of the Virgin Mary with the infant Jesus in her arms.

The spread of Egyptian opinions in Rome was so rapid under Augustus that it was felt to be of political importance, and it alarmed that prudent Emperor. The Romans by no means equalled the Greeks in their indifference to all religions and their toleration of all. Augustus made a law that no Egyptian ceremony should be allowed within either the city or the suburbs of Rome. But his law was without much effect, as at the same time Virgil, the court poet, was teaching the Egyptian millenium, or the resurrection of the dead when the thousand years are ended, and borrowing visions of the infernal regions from the Egyptian funereal papyri. Tiberius repeated the same law; but so little did it check the inroad of Egyptian superstition, that when the secular games were celebrated in Rome under the Emperor Claudius, the fabulous Egyptian bird, the phenix, was said to have arrived there. Nero openly patronized Apollonius of Tyana, who under the guidance of the Egyptian priests, and by the direct appointment of the Egyptian sacred tree, professed himself a teacher from heaven. Vespasian was so far pleased with the Egyptians, that when in Alexandria, he undertook with their approval to work miracles. His son, Domitian, wholly gave way to public opinion, and built in Rome a temple to Serapis, and another to Isis. Holy water was then brought from the Nile, for the use of the votaries in the temple of Isis in the Campus Martius; and a college of priests was maintained there with a splendour worthy of the Roman capital. The wealthy Romans wore upon their fingers gems engraved with the head of Hor-pi-krot, or *Horus the child*, called by them Harpocrates. (See Fig. 91.) The Museums of Europe contain many statues of the Egyptian gods made about this time by Roman artists, or perhaps by Greek artists in Rome, such as Jupiter-Serapis, Diana-Triformis, and Harpocrates. The Emperor Hadrian made his favourite Antinous into an Egyptian god; and Commodus had his head shaved as a priest of Isis, that he might more properly carry an Anubis-staff in the sacred processions in honour of the goddess. These circumstances are surely evidence enough of the readiness with which Rome under the Emperors shaped its Paganism after the Egyptian model, and prepare us to see without surprise that it looked to the same source for its views of Christianity. They prepare us for the remark of Origen, that all the neighbouring nations borrowed their religious rites and ceremonies from Egypt. (In Epist. ad Rom. ii. 495.)

Fig. 91.

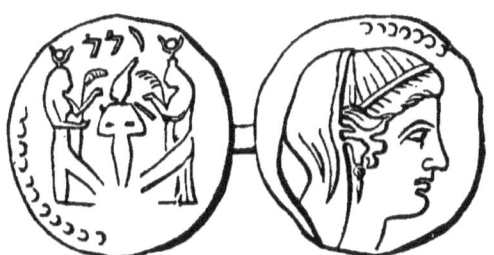

Egyptian gods on a coin of Malta.

CHRISTIANITY UNDER THE ROMAN EMPERORS.

CHRISTIANITY was first preached in Egypt by the Evangelist Mark, about thirty years after the Crucifixion. He had sailed with Barnabas to Cyprus (Acts xv. 39,) and thence probably went on to Alexandria. There he appointed, as the first of a succession of bishops, Ananiah, a Jew. The succeeding bishops seem to have been Greeks; so we may suppose that in Alexandria the religion made less progress with the Jews. Indeed, how fast Christianity spread during the first hundred years, among the sceptical Greeks of that city, is unknown. But at the end of that time we find full proof of how largely the Egyptians had embraced it by our finding the extent to which Egyptian opinions were received among the Christians. Egyptian mysticism, which had found such a ready entrance into the Greek and Roman Paganism, was not harmless when it came in contact with Christianity, whether it appeared in its own dress, or concealed under the guise of Alexandrian philosophy. From the very first we hear of it as an enemy to be shunned. The Apostle Paul wisely advises Timothy to avoid the antitheses of Gnosticism, or "the oppositions of Science falsely so called," (1 Tim. vi. 20). This Gnosticism was one of the forms in which we shall presently see mysticism uniting itself to Christianity in Alexandria. The Alexandrian opinions also appear in the Canonical

Epistle to the Hebrews. There Jesus is no longer the Teacher of a new Religion, as in the Gospels, but he acts as a mediator or advocate before the judge on behalf of mankind, as in the writings of the Son of Sirach, and as we have seen the Egyptian lesser gods acting—(in page 52)—not as a mediator to persuade the sinner to repent, but to persuade the Judge to forgive the sin. And his death is no longer that of a martyr to the great cause of regenerating his fellow creatures, but it is somewhat of an atoning sacrifice, made to propitiate the Judge, a doctrine which is shown on the sculpture in Fig. 70, page 50. These Alexandrian opinions were probably held by Apollos of Alexandria and Barnabas of Cyprus; and it was against some such "philosophy and vain deceit after the traditions of men," accompanied by a "voluntary humility and worshipping of angels," that Paul warns the Colossians (ii. 8; ii. 18; iv. 10). Soon afterwards were added to the Gospel of Matthew the first two chapters, giving to Jesus a miraculous birth, without an earthly father,—chapters of which we have historic information that they formed no part of the original Gospel, and which receive no support from the Gospels of Mark or John, or from any of the Epistles. The first two chapters also in Luke, the poetical chapters, though they allow Jesus to be the son of Joseph as well as of Mary, equally show their Egyptian origin. They give the circumstances attending his birth almost as if they were copied from the Egyptian sculpture in page 19, where we have seen the annunciation, the conception, the birth, and the adoration of the child, who afterwards became King Amunothph III.

In the year A.D. 160, a hundred years after Mark had

landed in Alexandria, we find four bishops governing as many Egyptian churches, which had adopted Christianity in some form or other. But whenever we hear of these Egyptian Christians, they are by the Greeks called Heretics. Numbers of them had readily consented to be baptised, and to fling away the belief in their old gods. But their new religious opinions had very little in common with the religion preached by Jesus and his apostles. Their Persian conquerors, though too tyrannical to win many minds from Polytheism, may yet have helped to undermine the belief in gods whose statues they had broken. The Greek conquerors, whose ridicule gained weight from their greater refinement, had further weakened the faith of some minds. Thus the Egyptians may have been somewhat prepared by their own doubts, though in a less degree than the Greeks and Romans, for the introduction of a new religion. But on the other hand, if the Egyptians had fewer theological doubts, they had more religious earnestness; and Christianity made its way, not only because the nations were opening their eyes to their intellectual errors, but because they were rising to an aim after more moral purity. Of the Pagan nations best known to us, the Egyptians were the most real believers in a resurrection from the dead, in a day of judgment, and in a future state of rewards and punishments. Through these doctrines, a wide door was open for the entrance of Christianity. Having been polytheists, they readily received Jesus Christ as a god in the place of some of their own; and that he should have been put to death by his enemies, could present no difficulty to their minds, as they had always been taught that their own god, Osiris, had died by an equally cruel death. A dying god was one of the great facts in their religious philosophy; and though they rejected their old gods, they could by no means so easily reject their old opinions. However, the despised Egyptians, on owning themselves Christians, and submitting to baptism, were at once received as equals into the society of the Greek Christians. They were raised, not legally, but socially, from slaves to be freemen. That any of the Greeks, their masters, should take the trouble to preach to them, to persuade them, to try to win them over to their own views of religion, was an honour which they had never before received; and as they owed it to Christianity, they cannot but have been led to look upon Christianity with favourable eyes.

The new religious opinions, however, of the Egyptians, had very little in common with the religion of the Apostles. They took such parts of the Gospel as suited their views, and could be fitted on to their old religion; but these rays of light they mixed up and buried under such a mass of superstition, that the Apostles themselves would not easily have recognised their own doctrines. The Christianity of the Egyptians, thus corrupted by the old Paganism of the country, shows itself in Alexandria first under the name of the Gnostic heresy. Gnosticism, that is *science* or *knowledge*, was the proud name given by its professors to a confused mixture of Greek philosophy and Egyptian superstition, to which they made no difficulty of adding Christianity. We learn something of it from the writers who oppose it, and something of it from their own sculptured gems, and something even from the Alexandrian coins of the emperors. As it was founded on a union between Greek, Egyptian, and Jewish opinions, it probably took its rise in Heliopolis, which was the most celebrated school before the building of Alexandria. But afterwards it spread from Alexandria to all the countries where Greek was spoken.

The peculiarities of the Gnostics very much show themselves in the attempt to explain the origin of evil—that never failing source of difficulty to philosophical reasoners. They held the Eastern opinion of two equal and co-eternal Beings, the one the author of good and the other of evil; that between these two there was an unceasing warfare, as between light and darkness, life and death, spirit and matter. These are the "oppositions of science, falsely so called," against which the Apostle Paul warned Timothy. The Gnostics held that matter was essentially evil, and consequently that God could not be its author. Even the Apocryphal Wisdom of Solomon says that God did not create death. The Supreme God and the Creator of the World were with the Gnostics two different Beings, and the latter was looked upon as the God of the Jews and the author of the Mosaic law. In this scheme, the Being with whom men have chiefly to do, either in this world or in the next, is the Creator of the World, the author of evil; and we see its connection with the old Egyptian opinions, by the engraved figures on the coins and gems. On Fig. 92, a coin of Hadrian, we see the Serpent of Good and the Serpent of Evil, both so common on the Egyptian monuments. The former is well distinguished by his swollen chest, but it is the latter, the Serpent of Evil,

Fig. 92.

SERPENT-WORSHIP.

that wears the crown of Osiris as judge of the dead. On a coin of Antoninus (Fig. 93,) the Serpent of Evil wears the head of Serapis, as the great god and judge, while on the engraved gem (Fig. 94,) the same serpent has a glory round its head, and

Fig. 93.

is entitled the Spirit of Evil, and underneath it is written

Fig. 94.

the magical word, Abrasax, *hurt me not*, an Egyptian word, which the Greeks made use of, as believing that the evil spirits were better acquainted with the Egyptian language than with the Greek. From thus representing the creator of the world under the form of a serpent, some of the Gnostics were named Ophitæ, or Serpent-worshippers; and in giving to this Being the name of Jao, a word written on his shield in Fig. 95, they declared him to be the Jah, or Jehovah of the Jews.

Another favourite doctrine of the Gnostics, was that of Æons, or spiritual beings, which proceeded from the Almighty, or rather into which the Almighty had in part divided himself. These were seven in number, of whom one was the Christ, who came down and dwelt in the body of Jesus. This opinion of a god dividing himself into several persons or characters, was part of the old Egyptian mythology, as we have seen in page 12; and these seven spirits, or Æons, we met with in the Greek translation of Isaiah, in page 61. The Gnostics, classing them with the Almighty as eight persons who together made only one God, worshipped them under the name of the Ogdoad, which is the earliest system of plurality in unity that we meet with among Christians of any sect. As the everlasting God was himself Eternity, so these angelic beings which proceeded from him were called Æons, *ages*, or limited periods of time, a name which seems to deny that they are of equal rank with the Eternal Being. And in the Epistle to the Hebrews, a book which shows much acquaintance with Alexandrian opinions, the Almighty is described as God who made the Æons or ages (chap. i. 2.) A later sect of Gnostics raised the number of Æons to thirty.

As the hostility of Matter to Spirit was the cause of all evil, the aim of Gnosticism was to purify its followers from the corruptions of Matter; and this was to be done by making them more perfect in Gnosis or mystical knowledge. And hence some thought that the body was to be kept under by the practice of self-denial, and by a rigid system of discipline; while others who had persuaded themselves that their Knowledge was everything, despised the distinctions of the moral law, and justly or unjustly were accused of gross vice.

These speculative and mystical opinions, which show themselves among the Christians in the form of Gnosticism, and among the Jews and Greek Pagans in the more modified form of New Platonism, took their rise in the School of Heliopolis, where the opinions of Jews, Greeks, and Egyptians had freely mingled, and had each made some change in the others. We have spoken of the changes introduced into Christianity by this mixing together of races; but the change in the old Egyptian religion shows itself in an approach towards the worship of One God. It was to be brought about by the help of various subtleties, without rejecting the old Polytheism, and chiefly by means of the doctrine of Plurality in Unity, by which, as we have before seen, they readily divided one God into several persons, and equally readily united several Gods into one person. Plutarch tells us that they worshipped Osiris, Isis, and Horus, under the form of a triangle, of which Horus was the shorter side. Of these representations of the Egyptian Trinity, we have many small specimens in our museums. (See Fig. 96.) He further tells us that they held that everything perfect had three parts, and therefore that their god of goodness made himself threefold, while their god of evil remained single.

Fig. 96.

Fig. 97.

On a coin of Trajan we see a winged sphinx, with three heads, leaning on a wheel, representing this threefold divinity. (See Fig. 97.) It reminds us of the Greek Cerberus, and which we might almost suppose to be the wicked Typhon, the accusing hippopotamus, who was one of the Cabeiri, if such an opinion did not contradict the rule quoted by Plutarch, that the god of evil remained single. It reminds us also of the living creatures of Ezekiel, chap. i., each of which had four heads and four wings, except that the creature described by the prophet had a wheel for each of the four faces. And indeed the same sphinx, leaning on

Fig. 98.

a wheel, was made use of by the Gnostic Christians, to represent Jesus Christ, as in the engraved gem, Fig. 98, where we see the white horse of the Book of Revelation vi. 2, "And he that sat on it had a bow, and a crown was given unto him, and he went forth conquering and to conquer," trampling down, as we see, the Dragon, or Serpent of Evil, while the figure of Victory presents to him the crown or diadem of royalty. A coin of the 11th year of Domitian represents another vision of the Book of Revelation, namely the Spirit of Death, in the form of a serpent, riding on the Pale Horse. See Fig. 99. As this was made after the Book of Revelation was written, so also may have been the gem, Fig. 98.

Fig. 99.

In the Book of Revelation, however, written in the year A.D. 69, we find many traces of the Gnostic or at least Egyptian opinions. One is in the seven spirits which were before the throne of God, in chap. i. 4, and which are again mentioned under the form of lamps, chap. iv. 5, and as eyes, in chap. v. 6. In page 76, we have shown that the writers of the Septuagint introduced these seven spirits into Isaiah xi. 2. Another Egyptian figure is in the war against the Dragon, or serpent of evil, in chap. xii., which is represented several times on the sarcophagus of Oimenepthah I., made perhaps B.C. 1200, and mentioned in page 43. The description of heaven, in chap. v. 5, the Judge on his throne, the four-and-twenty elders around the throne, the four living creatures with animals' heads, the Lamb standing before the throne, and the book-roll, would all seem in scenic effect to be copied from the Trial Scene described in page 41, though in its purpose it is very unlike. The horses tails ending in snakes heads we see on the gem, page 95.

The learned Greeks of Alexandria, whether Pagans or Christians, by no means held the superstitious Egyptian opinions, though certainly Greek philosophy had been not a little changed by having been cultivated for four centuries side by side with astrology, fortune-telling, priestly oracles, the Eleusinian mysteries, and the ceremonies in the great temple of Serapis. But the cold criticism and scepticism of the Museum may have driven many minds to feel more pleasure in credulity. Clemens shows some love of mysticism in his fondness for the sacred power of numbers, and Origen in his finding an allegory or second meaning hidden under the simple history of the Bible. And the praiseworthy wish to convert the Egyptians to Christianity led to describing the new religion in terms as near as possible to the old Paganism.

Clemens, in his words, though not so much in the meaning of his words, goes a long way to meet the opinions of the Egyptian Christians. He writes in favour of Gnosticism, *Science or Knowledge;* and though he is far from meaning the "Science falsely so called," spoken of by the Apostle Paul, which now goes by the name of Gnosticism, yet he cannot but have given some countenance to it, by adopting the language of his mystical neighbours. He describes every good man as having it in his power to rise from being a slave, to become a faithful servant of God, then a son, and at last a God walking in the flesh. Such words were understood figuratively, as they were meant, by the Platonic Christians of Alexandria; and it is only in sound that they agreed with the opinions of the

Egyptians who had accepted a belief in Jesus by considering him sometimes a god who had been put to death like Osiris, and sometimes a son of God in the same sense as their own Horus. But these words, though at first used figuratively, coloured the opinions of those who understood them literally.

If the Platonic Christians fancied that they were in any degree bringing over the Egyptians towards their own opinions by thus going forward to meet them, they were very much mistaken. The attempt to bridge over the gulf which separated the two opinions, did less to win the polytheists to Christianity than it did to make the Christianity of the country polytheistic. At the same time this concealing the difference between the two classes of believers, was very much driving away from Christianity the Jewish converts, who, like the Egyptians, though in an opposite direction, were equally straightforward in holding their opinions, and in the manner of expressing them.

Soon after the time of Clemens and Origen, the Alexandrian opinions again moved a step further towards the Egyptians. Dionysius, bishop of Alexandria, after first writing against the Gnostics, who said that there were thirty persons in the godhead, then writes to defend the new doctrine of a Trinity against Paul, the Syrian bishop, who said that God was One and undivided, and that Jesus was a man; and then again, Dionysius writes against Sabellius, bishop of Cyrene, who like Paul the Syrian, said that God was One and undivided, but unlike Paul, added that he had appeared on earth in the form of Jesus. Against these opposite opinions Dionysius defended a Trinity of Father, Son, and Holy Spirit, but in so doing he by no means comes up to the Egyptian standard. He distinctly denies to Jesus any higher rank than that of the first of created beings. His Trinity may be called the Arian Trinity, and is important as it marks one of the steps by which the Alexandrians were slowly fitting their mysticism to the Egyptian polytheism. The only advance which the Egyptians in return made towards the Greeks, was in the sect of the Docetæ, who were willing to get over the difficulty of a dying God, by their doctrine of apparitions. They said that Jesus died only in appearance, and hence their name of Docetæ, or *Seemers*. In the same way the Egyptians, five centuries earlier, had told Herodotus that Helen had been carried to Troy only in appearance, and that her real body had never been there. But the Greeks did not accept this view of the matter.

For the persecution of the Christians, both Greek and Egyptian, which began with the third century, we must seek an explanation in the state of the country in the years before the Egyptian rebellions. The Greek Christians had courted the Egyptians, had preached to them, had in part educated them, had raised them in their own eyes, and had made common cause with them, and thus made them discontented under their foreign rulers. This religious stir the government tried to stop, and the persecution of the Christians was as much political as religious. The Greeks, or the Roman government, which was very much in the hands of the Greeks, would probably never have been roused into intolerance unless the peace of the country had been threatened by an increased activity of mind among the Egyptians. The rebellion which followed made a yet further change in the religion. When the rebellion broke out, the union between Greek Christians and Egyptian Christians was broken; and when the rebellions were over, the Egyptians no longer acknowledged the Greeks as their religious partners.

From the death of Alexander Severus, in the year A.D. 235, till the accession of Constantine in A.D. 323, Egypt was torn to pieces by civil wars between rival emperors, by the invasion of the Syrians, and yet more by repeated rebellions of the native Egyptians against the power of Rome. While the disturbances continued Greek opinions were going fast out of favour with the Egyptians; the Greek mind was losing its supremacy, and Egyptian Christianity was henceforth to be for the most part under the guidance of Egyptians themselves. It was at the end of the third century, during the years of trouble, that the worship of the Persian Mithra, the god of the sun, was introduced into Egypt. In the Persian system of two gods, one good and the other wicked, Mithra was the god of goodness.

Fig. 100.

The symbol in his worship best known is the figure of a hero, in Phrygian cap and trowsers, mounted on a sinking bull, and stabbing it in sacrifice to the unseen god, while a dog licks up the blood from the wound. (See Fig. 100). This new worship received little favour in Egypt or Alexandria, and its ignorant followers were as ignorantly and wickedly accused of slaying their fellow citizens on the altars of the Persian god. The only part of this religion that gained a cordial welcome was the doctrine of Manicheism, a doctrine so closely akin to Gnosticism that it was hardly new. It was the doctrine of two supreme principles equally eternal and self-existent. One was mind and the other matter, one causing the happiness and the other the misery of men, one living in light and the other in darkness. This opinion, like the Antitheses of Gnosticism, had its rise in the difficulty of explaining the origin of sin, and of understanding how a merciful Creator could allow the existence of evil. The ignorant in all ages of Christianity have held the same opinion in one form or other, thinking that sin arose from the contrivances of a Devil, whom the All-powerful was not powerful enough to overcome, or else from the wickedness of the flesh itself. The Jews alone proclaimed that God created good, and God created evil. But the Jewish converts were now declared heretics by the more superstitious converts from Paganism, who were every year making the standard of orthodoxy conform more and more to Egyptian ignorance, and less to Greek intelligence. Hence Manichæism and the belief in a Devil took deep hold of the Egyptian Christians.

CHRISTIANITY
UNDER THE
BYZANTINE EMPERORS.

When quiet was re-established in Egypt by the Roman armies, after more than sixty years of civil troubles, it was found to be no longer the same country that it had been under the Antonines. The framework of society had been broken, the Greeks had lessened in numbers and still more in weight. Greek toleration of all religions and of all modes of thought then gave way to Egyptian more bigoted earnestness. The bright days of Egypt as a Greek kingdom ended with the rebellions against Gallienus, Aurelian, and Dioclesian. The native Egyptians and the old superstitions then rise again into notice, as Greek civilization sinks around them. The building of Constantinople, and the removal of the seat of government from Rome to that new Greek city, yet further lessened the numbers, and thus the rank of the Greeks in Alexandria. Among the Christians, the more superstitious Egyptians, whose religion was still polytheism under a Christian form, as being now the more numerous, are able in their turn to call the Greek Christians heretics. Then began the celebrated Arian controversy, as to whether Jesus Christ were a God or a created being; and the same intolerance, which ten centuries earlier would not allow the Libyans to eat beef, is now uneasy at there being two opinions about the miraculous birth of the Saviour. The opinions of Arius were the same as those of the late bishop Dionysius, that Jesus was the First of Created Beings. But what was orthodoxy before the rebellions, while the Greeks were able to treat the Egyptians as slaves, was heresy since the Egyptians had found out their weight and power; and the young and able Athanasius, a Greek deacon in the Alexandrian church, rose into importance by taking the Egyptian side in the controversy.

It was not in the first instance seen that the dispute was in reality a political struggle between the Egyptians and the Greeks, but it took the form of a religious argument as to whether Jesus was an uncreated being of one substance with God, or was inferior to the Father. The quarrel in Alexandria unsettled the faith of the world, so much was that city a guide both to the east and west in matters of religion; and the Emperor Constantine was persuaded to call a council of bishops to meet at Nicæa, in Asia Minor, to settle the question. Unfortunately the decline of civilization and the increase of ignorance, during the last two centuries, had been as great in Greece and Italy as in Alexandria. The civil wars between rival emperors, the licence of the soldiers, the inroads of the barbarians, and the progress of despotism, had crushed free thought and genius everywhere. The Roman or western half of the known world was wholly without a writer of any kind, except in the ranks of the prejudiced theologians; and in the Greek or Eastern provinces what little learning or cultivation remained was chiefly to be found in Alexandria. Hence when the creed of Christendom was to be settled by the votes of the bishops, after

Egyptian superstition had already gained a strong footing in Alexandria, any purer or more simple views of Christianity stood little chance of holding their ground in an assembly of divines summoned from yet wider and more ignorant provinces.

At Nicæa, as is usually the case in an assembly of divines, the more superstitious talked down and frowned down the more reasonable. The Emperor sided with the Egyptians, which may be explained by what we have before seen, because Greece and Rome had been used to look up to Egypt as their teacher in religion; and he had lately, on building Constantinople, received from Alexandria fifty copies of Church Lessons, for the use of his new churches. The Egyptian opinions, supported by the eloquence and earnestness of the young Athanasius, the spokesman of the Egyptian bishops, prevailed. He drew up the celebrated form of words, now known by the name of the Nicene Creed, as a statement of the opinions which the Egyptians contended for; and the council ended their labours by ordering everybody to receive it as the true Christian faith.

The controversy was by no means at once settled by this decree. When Constantine saw that the quarrel was more political than religious, he took the other side of the question, and joined the Greeks; and Egypt continued almost in rebellion on a point of controversial theology, during the reigns of Constantine, Constantius, Julian, Jovian, and Valens. For forty years Athanasius, the darling hero of the Egyptians, was able to defy the power of the Emperors, and after his death peace was restored only on the accession of Theodosius, who took the side of the Egyptians, and

Egypt. That large class of the population which a few years before formed the priesthood of the old temples were now Christian monks. They were all zealous supporters of Athanasius, and all earnest against the Arian opinions of the Greeks. For their use, three Egyptian translations of the Bible were made, one into the language used in the Western half of the Delta, called Coptic, a second into that of the Eastern half, called Bashmuric, and a third into the Thebaic, for the use of Upper Egypt and Nubia. They readily fitted the old temples to the new religion. Their opinions had undergone but small change. On the rock temple of Kneph, opposite Abou Simbel, they painted the figure of the Saviour, with a glory round his head upon the ceiling, and thus it became a Christian church. (See Fig. 101). The great court-yard of the temple of Medinet Abou, at Thebes, was used as a

Fig. 101.

cathedral church dedicated to St. Athanasius. In some cases, they removed from before their eyes the memorials of the old superstition, by covering up the sculptures on the walls with mud from the Nile, and white plaster. In other cases, they contented themselves with making a slight change in the sculpture, as at the temple of Seboua, in Nubia, where they painted the figure of the Apostle Peter over that of the old god of the temple, and the sculpture now represents King Ramesis II. presenting his offerings to the Christian Saint. (See Fig. 102).

By the burst of enthusiasm in favour of Athanasius, the Nicene creed became the received religion of all native Egyptians, and

Fig 102.

beyond them of those Alexandrians, who aimed at rising into importance by taking the popular side in the quarrel. Arianism on the other hand, even when supported by the weak government of the emperor, lost ground rapidly, and it soon took refuge in the fortified camps of the Greek soldiers. A church was dedicated to the Arian bishop George, within the walls of the strong castle of Babylon, opposite Memphis, and another at Ptolemais, where the Greek garrison collected the toll of the Thebaid, and where the modern village yet bears his name and is called allowed them in their turn to persecute the more enlightened Arian Greeks. From that time forward the Christianity of the superstitious Egyptians became the Christianity of the majority in Alexandria, and after a time, with very few variations, the Christianity of the greater part of the world.

The aim of the Nicene Creed was to require everybody to acknowledge that Jesus Christ was a God, in such clear and forcible terms as to turn out of the Church all who would not follow the Egyptians in the mystical opinions which they had introduced, so that there should be no escape for those who believed in one only God, and who gave any whatever lower rank to the Saviour. It declares that there is one God, the Maker of all things, and yet that the one Lord Jesus Christ, was not made; that he also was very God of very God, and was yet crucified by Pontius Pilate; that he had been previously incarnate by the Holy Ghost of the Virgin Mary and made man, although of one substance with the Father. All this carried with it no contradiction to the mind of the Egyptians. They were used to being told and believing that two Gods could be one God. They were used to hear of a God being put to death, as they had always held that Osiris, though a god, had been put to death. They were used to hear of children being born of an earthly mother and having no earthly father, as they held that many of their kings were so born, being incarnate by the god Amun-Ra. But Athanasius did not introduce into his creed any Egyptian mysticism to support, nor did he try to explain away its inconsistency by any play upon words. The Nicene creed does not mention the Trinity nor the two natures of Christ, but leaves the contradictions stated in the boldest terms. The well-known Athanasian creed, in which an explanation of the difficulties has been attempted, is supposed to have been written two or three hundred years later, and the name of the great Alexandrian bishop has been given to it, either dishonestly or because it was thought to represent his opinions. This later creed states that though "the Father is God, the Son is God, and the Holy Ghost is God, yet they are not three Gods but one God." This is the Egyptian doctrine of plurality in unity, which is represented in numerous sculptures and explained in pages 13, 95. It then asserts the two natures of Christ, that he is both "perfect God and perfect man." This was meant to get over the difficulty of a dying God which had been ridiculed by Xenophanes, in the case of Osiris, five centuries before the Christian era; when he told the Egyptians that if Osiris was a man they should not worship him, and if he was a god they need not lament his sufferings. But this Athanasian creed, though setting forth the Egyptian opinions, was an offspring of the Latin church, and it is very doubtful whether it would have been wholly approved of by Athanasius. The Egyptians had raised Mary the wife of Joseph almost into a goddess, at least into "the mother of God," who had imparted no portion of human nature to her son; they denied the two natures of Christ, and clung faithfully to the words of their own Nicene creed, which declared that he was "of one substance with the Father."

It was during these years of civil trouble and political agitation that Christianity, or at least a form of religion which called itself Christian, spread over the whole of founders, were sent to St. Jerome at Rome, to be by him translated into Latin, for the use of these settlers in the Thebaid. The two countries shaped their opinions so nearly in the same mould that when St. Jerome visited Egypt, he found the church there holding what he called the true Roman faith. Two at least of these teachers of monastic discipline were clearly Egyptians, not Greeks. Their names, Pachomius, or Pa-chem, *a priest of the god Chem*, and Oresiesis, or Hor-se-isis, *Horus the son of Isis*, even without the evidence of the foregoing pages, might have led us to suppose that the source of their theology, both for themselves and for the Theban monasteries under their rule, was as much Pagan as Christian.

The closeness with which Western Europe followed Egypt may be seen even in smaller matters. St. Ambrose, Archbishop of Milan, calls Jesus "the good Scarabæus, who rolled up before him the hitherto unshapen mud of our bodies," thus giving to him one of the names and characters of the god Horus, who is pictured as a scarabæus with a ball of mud between his feet. (See Fig. 103). The ball, which usually means the sun, would seem to have sometimes meant the sins of mankind; and the goddesses Isis and Nephthys are often represented as rolling the same ball before them. St. Augustin also during the greater part of his life was a Manichæan, and held the Gnostic opinion of a god of goodness and a god of evil; and he was so far an admirer of the Egyptians, or at least of their practice of making mummies, as to say that they were the only Christians who really and fully believed in a future resurrection from the dead.

Fig. 103.

If St. Jerome, when noting the religious agreement between Rome and Egypt, really fancied that in anything whatever Rome had been the teacher, he had read history to very little purpose. But Rome and Egypt then held the same views of Christianity, which have since been known as the opinions of the Roman church, and which were at the time rejected as too superstitious by many of the more learned bishops of Constantinople, Asia Minor, and Syria, who for the time held back from the Athanasian opinions. Hence arose the separate establishment of the Greek church, which for a short time was Arian, and which from political causes has ever since been disjoined from the Roman church. Political causes also, arising from the disturbed state of the world in the fifth century, presently separated Egypt from Italy; and then the Coptic and the Roman church ceased to hold so exactly the same opinions. As Greek intelligence offered every year less check to Egyptian ignorance, the Coptic church became yet more superstitious; though fortunately for Rome, that city was no longer in danger of being led to follow.

The churches of Constantinople and Greece, with the Greek churches of Asia Minor and Syria, did not, as we have said, at first move towards the Egyptian opinions quite so fast as Italy and the West. But the change from the earlier faith was presently quickened in the East by political circumstances. On the death of the Emperor Valens in A. D. 379, Theodosius, a general who had been born in Spain, and brought up in Western Christianity, was made Emperor of Constantinople and the East. The disturbed state of his dominions called for the strong arm of military despotism; and Theodosius required the church by the Arabs Geergeh. St. George became a favourite saint with the Greeks in Egypt, and in those few spots where the Greek soldiers were masters of the churches, this Arian and unpopular bishop was often painted on the walls, riding triumphantly on horseback and slaying the great serpent or dragon of Athanasian error.

At this time a marked separation was taking place between the opinions of Constantinople, the chief seat of the Greek church, and those of Egypt and Rome. The more civilized Constantinople held aloof for the present from the more superstitious Egypt as its religious guide. But the case was far otherwise with Rome. Since the building of Constantinople, and the removal of the seat of government to that city, no political quarrel separated Rome from Egypt. Pagan Rome ever since the union of the two countries under Augustus, except when interrupted by the rebellions, had been eagerly copying the superstitions of Egypt, and Christian Rome still followed the same course.

When in the reign of Constantine the country was quiet, the intercourse between the Egyptian and the Roman churches was renewed under still more favourable circumstances, because the city of Alexandria had become more Egyptian and less Greek than ever it had been before. Constans, the next Emperor of Rome, openly gave his support to Athanasius when in rebellious disobedience to Constantius his own sovereign; and the opinions of Athanasius received the support of the whole Roman church. At the end of the third century Hesychius of Alexandria, had published a new edition of the Greek Bible with a corrected text, and such was the credit of

Alexandria, as the chief seat of Christian learning, that all distant churches sent there for copies of the scriptures. When Constans wanted copies of the Greek scriptures for Rome, he sent for them to Alexandria and received the approved text from Athanasius. In this, a matter of learning belonging to the last century, the Roman Emperor acted wisely, but in the matter of religious opinions, the case was far otherwise. Alexandria in the fourth century was very different from that Alexandria which had earned its high character for criticism and scholarship, though the change in the eyes of the Roman church was a change for the better; and they were equally pleased to import from the same city Alexandrian manuscripts and Egyptian superstitions. All Christendom was copying the monastic institutions of the Thebaid. Italy and the West acknowledged Egypt as their best instructress in all ecclesiastical matters; and the approval which they gave to the ecclesiastical institutions could hardly have been yielded so cordially, unless they at the same time gave a full approval to the religious opinions. As the Egyptians excelled all other Christians in the practice of self-denial and fleshly mortification, so their religion was naturally thought the most pleasing to God, and their theological views the soundest. Natives of Italy, not content with living in their own monasteries under the strict Theban rules, flocked into Egypt to place themselves under the severe discipline, and to learn the opinions of the ignorant Egyptian monks. As these Latin monks did not understand either Coptic or Greek, they found some difficulty in regulating their lives with the wished for exactness; and the rules of Pacomius, of Theodorus, and of Oresiesis, the most celebrated of the to give the same obedience to his simple will that he received from the army. He at once dismissed the Arian patriarch of Constantinople, and ordered all the clergy to be turned out of their churches if they would not receive the Nicene creed. He summoned a council of bishops to meet at Constantinople, for the purpose of having the Nicene creed declared to be the creed of the church of the whole world. He did not summon to it either the Egyptian bishops or the Western bishops; they already held the Nicene faith. He summoned only the Eastern church, and in that council under his orders, the Nicene creed was re-enacted forty-five years after the Arians had been allowed to re-enter the church. The Council of Constantinople also added to the creed the clauses which declare the Holy Spirit to be a person who ought to be worshipped equally with God and Jesus, leaving the Nicene creed very nearly as it is now read, and thus for the first time establishing the Trinity as now understood by the so called orthodox Christians,

The book trade of Alexandria gave to the Egyptian opinions a great importance in the Christian world. All the oldest and best manuscripts of the Greek Bible now remaining were written by Alexandrian penmen, that of Paris, that of the Vatican, that of Cambridge, that of the British Museum, and that from Mount Sinai, now in Russia. In Alexandria were made the Ethiopic version and probably the early Latin version. The Armenian version and the old Syriac version were corrected in Alexandria, from the most approved and newest Greek text. These are strong proofs of the rank which that city held and of its power to guide the opinions of foreign

Christians. Nor were corn and books the only products which other countries received from Egypt, either as tribute or by purchase.

About the middle of the fourth century there was a general digging up of the bodies of the most celebrated Christians of former ages to heal the diseases and strengthen the faith of the living. The tombs of Egypt, crowded with mummies which had lain there for centuries, could of course furnish relics more easily than most countries; and Constantinople then received from Egypt a quantity of bones which were supposed to be those of the martyrs slain in the Pagan persecutions. The archbishop John Chrisostome received them gratefully, and though himself smarting under the reproach that he was not orthodox, according to the measure of the superstitious Egyptians, he thanks God that Egypt which sent forth its corn to feed its hungry neighbours, could also send the bodies of so many martyrs to sanctify their churches. And Gregory of Nazianzum a little before had remarked that Egypt was the most Christ-loving of countries, and adds with true simplicity that wonderful to say, after having so lately worshipped bulls, goats, and crocodiles, it was now teaching the world the worship of the Trinity in the truest form.

Fig. 104.—Isis rising heliacally.

LIST OF WOODCUTS.

FIG.
1. The Winged Sun as vault of heaven.
2. Amun-Ra.
3. Mandoo.
4. Hapimou, the Nile.
5. Chem.
6. Kneph.
7. Pthah.
8. Neith.
9. Isis.
10. Athor.
11. Pasht.
12. Thoth.
13. Osiris.
14. Horus.
15. Anubis.
16. Nephthys.
17. Typhon.
18. Chonso.
19. Seb.
20. Serapis.
21. Amun-Ra, Maut, and Chonso.
22. Horus between Isis and Nephthys.
23. Rameses III. between Isis and Nephthys.
24. Apis.
25. Uræus or Asp.
26. Scarabæus.

FIG.
27. The title of Zera, *Son of the Sun*.
28. The Birth of Amunothph III.
29. The Tree of life and knowledge.
30. A Column from Temple of Karnak.
31. Plan of temple of Errebck.
32. Portico of the same.
33. Plan of temple of Seboua.
34. Plan of temple of Sarbout el Kadem.
35. Portico of Coutra Latopolis.
36. Portico of Tentyra restored.
37. Plan of the Memnonium.
38. View and plan of temple of Philæ.
39. Priest squatting on the ground.
40. Crown of Upper Egypt.
41. Crown of Lower Egypt.
42. Double crown.
43. Stone head-rest.
44. Border of flower and fruit.
45, 46, 47. Emblems of Urim and Thummim.
48. The Ark.
49. The Singer or Musician.
50. The Prophet.
51. The Scribe.
52. A Priestess.
53. A Priest carrying an hour-glass.

116 LIST OF WOODCUTS.

FIG.
54. Statue of a Pastopharus or Shrine-bearer.
55. Procession of sacred boats.
56. Serpent on a standard.
57. Divining cup.
58. Priest with leopard skin.
59. Votive Pyramid.
60. The King, Queen, their son, and Priests sacrificing.
61. Pyramid of Chofo.
62. Plan and section of tomb.
63. King embracing a god.
64. The Conquerors of the great serpent.
65. Mummy with three cases.
66. Four lesser gods of the dead.
67. Isis and Nephthys grieving for the dead.
68. Anubis laying out a mummy.
69. Basin copied from a water-tank.
70. The Trial of the dead.
71. Gods mediating for the dead.
72. Gods sacrificed as an atonement.
73. Soul returning to the mummy.
74. Animal body and spiritual body.
75. Enemies under the soles of the shoes.
Page 57. Nilometer Landmark.
Fig. 76. Neith with outstretched wings as vault of heaven.
77. Pigmy Pthah.
78. The same with club.
79. The same, Cabeiri and Pit of fire
80. King appeasing the Cabeiri.

FIG.
81. Chiun with Chem and Ranpo.
„ Anaita worshipped.
82. Fire and water offered.
Page 69. Tomb with an arch.
83. Sun worship by Persian Satrap.
84. Egyptian Ra altered with rays and hands.
Page 72. Name of Thaomra.
Fig. 85. Eleusinian basket and serpent.
Page 82. Apis on coins of Cyprus.
Fig. 86. Horus as vault of heaven.
87. Osiris—Horus—Ra.
88. Pthah—Horus—Ra.
89. Horus as a child.
90. Isis nursing Horus.
91. Harpocrates.
Page 87. Egyptian gods in Malta.
Fig. 92. Serpents of good and evil.
93. Serapis as serpent of evil.
94. Serpent of Evil with glory.
95. Serpent of Evil as Jao.
96. Triangular gem.
97. Trinity as a Spinx.
98. Conqueror over Evil on horseback
99. Spirit of Evil on horseback.
100. Mithra.
101. Figure of Jesus in a temple.
102. St. Peter worshipped by Rameses II.
103. Scarabæus and ball of dirt.
104. Isis rising heliacally.

BOOKS PUBLISHED

BY

JOHN RUSSELL SMITH,

36, Soho Square, London.

THE EGYPTIAN ANTIQUITIES in the British Museum described. By SAMUEL SHARPE, Esq., Author of the "History of Ancient Egypt," &c. Post 8vo, *with many woodcuts, cloth.* 5s

" The book is illustrated with woodcuts from the excellent drawings of Mr. Bonomi, and it will doubtless be of great service to visitors who wish to form some correct ideas concerning the miscellaneous collection of statues, tables, coffins, mummies, and oddities innumerable, which are here gathered together."—*Literary Gazette.*

"In a convenient and portable volume the author of the "History of Egypt" imparts the exact sort of information which visitors to the Museum crave to possess, while even advanced scholars may refer with advantage to his careful arrangement of the historic series of antiquities according to their chronological order."—*Spectator.*

" We strongly counsel every one who desires to obtain a true knowledge of the Egyptian department of the Museum to lose no time in obtaining this cheap and excellent volume."—*Daily News.*

THE NEW TESTAMENT. Translated from Griesbach's Text. By SAMUEL SHARPE, Author of the "History of Egypt," &c., 5th Edition, 12mo, pp. 412, *well printed, cloth, red edges.* 1s 6d

The aim of the translator has been to give the meaning and idiom of the Greek as far as possible in English words. The book is printed in paragraphs (the verses of the authorised version are numbered in the margin), the speeches by inverted commas, and the quotations from the " Old Testament" in Italics, those passages which seem to be poetry in a smaller type. It is entirely free from any motive to enforce doctrinal points. Five large impressions of the volume sufficiently test its value. The price now places it within the reach of all classes.

"Upon the whole we must admit that Mr. Sharpe's is the most correct English version in existence, either of the whole of or any portion of the New Testament." — THE ECCLESIASTIC, quoted with approval by the ENGLISH CHURCHMAN, 18th Dec. 1862.

THE PHARAOH OF THE EXODUS. An Examination of the Modern Systems of Egyptian Chronology, by D. W. Nash, F.L.S., Author of "Taliesin," &c., 8vo, *with frontispiece of the Egyptian Calendar, from the ceiling of the Ramesseum at Thebes, cloth.* 12s

MEMORIALS OF KING ALFRED, being Essays on the History and Antiquities of England during the Ninth Century, the Age of King Alfred. By various authors. Edited and in part written by the Rev. Dr. GILES. Royal 8vo, pp. 384, *plates of Alfred's Jewel, his Coins, etc. etc., cloth.* 7s 6d

BOOKS PUBLISHED BY JOHN RUSSELL SMITH.

THE WRITINGS OF THE CHRISTIANS OF THE SECOND CENTURY, namely, Athenagoras, Tatian, Theophilus, Hermias, Papias, Aristides, Quadratus, &c., collected and first translated complete, by the Rev. Dr. GILES. 8vo, *cloth.* 7s 6d
    Designed as a continuation of Abp. Wake's *Apostolical Epistles,* which are those of the first century.

HISTORY OF THE NONJURORS: their Controversies and Writings, with Remarks on some of the Rubricks in the Book of Common Prayer. By the Rev. THOS. LATHBURY, M.A. Thick 8vo, *cloth.* 6s (pub 14s)

HISTORY OF THE CONVOCATION OF THE CHURCH OF ENGLAND, from the Earliest Period to the Year 1742. By the Rev. THOS. LATHBURY, M.A. *Second Edition, with considerable Additions,* thick 8vo, *cloth.* 5s (pub 12s)

HISTORY OF PARISH REGISTERS IN ENGLAND, and Registers of Scotland, Ireland the Colonies, Episcopal Chapels in and about London, the Geneva Register of the Protestant Refugees, with Biographical Notes, &c. By J. SOUTHERDEN BURN. *Second Edition, enlarged,* 8vo, *cloth.* 10s 6d

A GLOSSARY; or, Collection of Words, Phrases, Customs, Proverbs, &c., illustrating the Works of English Authors, particularly Shakespeare and his contemporaries. By ROBERT NARES, Archdeacon of Stafford, &c. A New Edition, with considerable Additions, both of Words and Examples. By JAMES O. HALLIWELL, F.R.S., and THOMAS WRIGHT, M.A., F.S.A. 2 thick vols. 8vo, *cloth.* £1. 8s
    The Glossary of Archdeacon Nares is by far the best and most useful work we possess for explaining and illustrating the obsolete language, and the customs and manners of the sixteenth and seventeenth centuries, and it is quite indispensable for the readers of the literature of the Elizabethan period. The additional words and examples are distinguished from those in the original text by a † prefixed to each. The work contains between *five and six thousand* additional examples, the result of original research, not merely supplementary to Nares, but to all other compilations of the kind.

DICTIONARY OF ARCHAIC AND PROVINCIAL WORDS, Obsolete Phrases, Proverbs, and Ancient Customs, from the Reign of Edward I. By JAMES ORCHARD HALLIWELL, F.R.S., F.S.A., &c., 2 vols. 8vo, *containing upwards of* 1000 *pages closely printed in double columns, cloth, a new and cheaper edition.* 15s
    It contains above 50,000 words (embodying all the known scattered Glossaries of the English language), forming a complete key for the reader of our old Poets, Dramatists, Theologians, and other authors, whose works abound with allusions of which explanations are not to be found in ordinary Dictionaries and books of reference. Most of the principal Archaisms are illustrated by examples selected from early inedited MSS. and rare books, and by far the greater portion will be found to be original authorities.

RETROSPECTIVE REVIEW (New Series); consisting of Criticisms upon, Analysis, of, and Extracts from, curious, useful, valuable, and scarce Old Books. 8vo, Vols. I. and II. *(all printed) cloth.* 10s 6d (original price £1 1s)
    These two volumes from a good companion to the old series of the *Retrospective,* in 16 vols.; the articles are of the same length and character.

LIFE, PROGRESSES, & REBELLION OF JAMES, DUKE OF MONMOUTH, &c., to his Capture and Execution, with a full account of the "Bloody Assize," under Judge Jefferies, and copious Biographical Notices. By GEORGE ROBERTS. 2 vols. post 8vo, *plates and cuts, cloth.* 7s 6d (original price £1. 4s)

  Two very interesting volumes, particularly so to those connected with the West of England. Lord Macaulay admits his indebtedness to the work.

ANECDOTES AND CHARACTERS OF BOOKS AND MEN. Collected from the Conversation of Mr. Pope and other eminent Persons of his Time. By the Rev. JOSEPH SPENCE. With Notes, Life, &c. by S. W. SINGER. The second edition, fcap. 8vo, *portrait, elegantly printed by Whittingham, cloth.* 6s

——— LARGE PAPER, *(for the connoisseur of books).* Post 8vo, *cloth.* 7s 6d

  "The 'Anecdotes' of kind-hearted Mr. Spence, the Friend of Pope, is one of the best books of *ana* in the English language."—*Critic.*

THE TABLE TALK OF JOHN SELDEN. With a Biographical Preface and Notes by S. W. SINGER. Fcap. 8vo, *third edition, portrait, cloth.* 5s

——— LARGE PAPER *(for the connoisseur of choice books).* Post 8vo, *cloth.* 7s 6d

  "Nothing can be more interesting than this little book, containing a lively picture of the opinions and conversations of one of the most eminent scholars and most distinguished patriots England has produced. There are few volumes of its size so pregnant with sense, combined with the most profound learning; it is impossible to open it without finding some important fact or discussion, something practically useful and applicable to the business of life. Coleridge says, 'There is more weighty bullion sense in this book than I ever found in the same number of pages in any uninspired writer.' . . Its merits had not escaped the notice of Dr. Johnson, though in politics opposed to much it inculcates, for in reply to an observation of Boswell, in praise of the French Ana, he said, 'A few of them are good, but we have one book of that kind better than any of them—Selden's Table Talk.'"—*Mr. Singer's Preface.*

NOTES ON ANCIENT BRITAIN AND THE BRITONS. By the Rev. W. BARNES, author of the "Philological Grammar," "Anglo-Saxon Delectus," "Dorset Dialect," &c. Fcap. 8vo, *cloth.* 3s

  "Mr. Barnes has given us the result of his Collections for a Course of Lectures on this subject, and has produced a series of Sketches of the Ancient Britons, their language, laws, and modes of life, and of their social state as compared with that of the Saxons, which will be read with considerable interest."—*Notes and Queries.*

BRITANNIC RESEARCHES; or, New Facts and Rectifications of Ancient British History. By the Rev. BEALE POSTE, M.A. 8vo, (pp. 448), *with engravings, cloth.* 15s

  "The author of this volume may justly claim credit for considerable learning, great industry, and, above all, strong faith in the interest and importance of his subject. . . On various points he has given us additional information, and afforded us new views, for which we are bound to thank him. The body of the book is followed by a very complete index, so as to render reference to any part of it easy; this was the more necessary, on account of the multifariousness of the topics treated, the variety of persons mentioned, and the many works quoted."—*Athenæum,* Oct. 8, 1853.

BOOKS PUBLISHED BY JOHN RUSSELL SMITH.

BRITANNIA ANTIQUA, or Ancient Britain brought within the Limits of Authentic History. By the Rev. BEALE POSTE. 8vo, pp. 386, *map, cloth.* 14s

A Sequel to the foregoing work.

CELTIC INSCRIPTIONS ON GAULISH AND BRITISH COINS, intended to supply materials for the Early History of Great Britain, with a Glossary of Archaic Celtic Words, and an Atlas of Coins. By the Rev. BEALE POSTE. 8vo, *many engravings, cloth.* 10s 6d

THE PILGRIM FATHERS.—Collections concerning the Church or Congregation of Protestant Separatists formed at Scrooby, in North Nottinghamshire, in the Time of James I., the Founders of New Plymouth, the Parent Colony of New England. By the Rev. JOSEPH HUNTER, F.S.A., *and an Assistant Keeper of Her Majesty's Records.* 8vo, *cloth.* 8s

This work contains some very important particulars of these personages, and their connections previously to their leaving England and Holland, which were entirely unknown to former writers, and have only recently been discovered, through the indefatigable exertions of the author. Prefixed to the volume are some beautiful Prefatory Stanzas by Richard Monckton Milnes, Esq., M.P.

ANGLO-SAXON DELECTUS; serving as a first Class-Book to the Language. By the Rev. W. BARNES, B.D., of St. John's College, Cambridge. 12mo, *cloth.* 2s 6d

COMPENDIOUS ANGLO-SAXON AND ENGLISH DICTIONARY, by the Rev. J. BOSWORTH, D.D., F.R.S., &c., *Anglo-Saxon Professor in the University of Oxford.* 8vo, *closely printed in treble columns.* 12s

GUIDE TO THE ANGLO-SAXON TONGUE; on the Basis of Professor Rask's Grammar; to which are added Reading Lessons, in Verse and Prose, with Notes for the use of Learners, by J. E. VERNON, B.A., Oxon. 12mo, *cloth.* 5s

"Mr. Vernon has, we think, acted wisely in taking Rask for his model; but let no one suppose from the title that the book is merely a compilation from the work of that philologist. The accidence is abridged from Rask, with constant revision, correction and modification; but the syntax a most important portion of the book, is original, and is compiled with great care and skill; and the latter half of the volume consists of a well chosen selection of extracts from Anglo-Saxon writers, in prose and verse, for the practice of the student, who will find great assistance in reading them, from the grammatical notes with which they are accompanied, and from the glossary which follows them. This volume, well studied, will enable any one to read with ease the generality of Anglo-Saxon writers; and its cheapness places it within the reach of every class. It has our hearty recommendation."—*Literary Gazette.*

TIW, or a View of the Roots and Stems of the English as a Teutonic Tongue. By the Rev. W. BARNES, B.D., Author of the "Dorset Poems," "Philological Grammar," "Anglo-Saxon Delectus," &c. Fcap. 8vo, *cloth.* 5s

"I hold that my primary roots are the roots of all the Teutonic languages; and if my view is the true one it must ultimately be taken up by the German and other Teutonic grammarians, and applied to their languages."—*The Author.*

BOWDEN & BRAWN, Printers, 13, Princes Street, Little Queen Street, Holborn.

www.ingramcontent.com/pod-product-compliance
Lightning Source LLC
Chambersburg PA
CBHW030401170426
43202CB00010B/1451